# The Basketball Chronicles

# of Mister Jennings

Keith Mister Jennings

# Contents

# Introduction

What does basketball mean to me? Basketball is life. It was my first true love before women entered my life. The game of basketball is so complex, but for me it's so simple. The objective is to win, win every time you play! That's what I tried to do. I like winning streaks, not losing streaks. I'm the type of player that will challenge myself, then I'm going to challenge my teammates and I can't wait to challenge my opponents. I love to play basketball. I love to watch basketball. I love to talk basketball. I love to teach basketball and I love to coach basketball. Basketball is my safe haven. I can go to a court anywhere in the world, inside or outside, dribble and shoot and be at peace with myself no matter what I'm going through, and I've been through a lot. I know that God has put me here for a reason, and one of those reasons is to do my best with this game of basketball.

Keith "Mister" Jennings

My story is different, but I'm sure every small player that wanted to become a professional basketball player can relate to what I had to go through. I'm 5'7" and there are so many small basketball players that get overlooked because of their size. I want to be the voice for those players. I was blessed by God with the talent and love to be a basketball player. Through God's grace and timing, basketball has shown me parts of the world that I would've never visited and the great support that I received from my family and friends will never be forgotten or taken for granted…dream big, work for it and see what happens!

Growing up in the Jennings' household during basketball season was something I loved and respected. Basketball in the morning, basketball in the evening, basketball at night, basketball in the house, basketball in the gyms, basketball at the dunk courts, basketball on television, basketball movies, basketball without a basketball, I just couldn't get enough and then it turned into a memory bank. Memories of family basketball, memories of high school basketball, memories of college basketball, memories of the NBA, memories of European basketball, memories of good games, bad games, great games, and injuries. If the good outweighs the bad you'll be happy to share your story with anyone that asks. You have to understand that a lot of people never gave me a chance. My family believed in me and I believed in myself, and I worked so hard I get chills just thinking about it. The memories don't stop until you stop.

I found out very quickly that short basketball players need to be special. Looking back on it, I realized that the short players that I liked were special. Mugsy Boges was 5'3", Spud Webb was 5'7" and could dunk (he won the NBA dunk contest back in the day), Calvin Murphy was a flat out scorer, and the list goes on and on. At this present time there are only 10 basketball players under 6' that have played 3 years or more in the NBA. I felt like I was special because I played basketball on all major levels: high school, college, NBA and European professional basketball. I'm going to take you through a series of events that I believe gave me the opportunity to not only have my basketball dreams come true, but to also be able to make money doing something I love.

Have you ever been to a place where you feel at peace with yourself? If you haven't, I hope you find it before your time on this earth is done. My peace is basketball. It doesn't matter what is going on in my life, I can grab a basketball, find a rim and the rim doesn't even have to have nets. I'll forget everything and just play. It's a great feeling. I believe dreams come true. Mine did and yours can too. You just need to be patient, work hard, don't listen to the negative people (haters), and believe in your own abilities. I did. I had to deal with all of those things and it shaped me to be the man that I am today.

# Chapter 1:
# Family and Friends Are Like Teammates

It all starts with my mom and dad. I like to think of them as the head coach and assistant. I won't say which is which, but they're the ones that brought me into this world and as my dad would often say, "I brought you in to this world and I'll take you out." I really believed him so he didn't have to worry about me disrespecting him, and my mom held it down in a way that I knew better than to think about disrespecting her. All in all, we didn't have a lot of money, but we had a lot of love. My oldest sister Sherry lived in Alabama so I didn't get to see her until the summers. My oldest sister lived at home. Karen, or should we say KK, taught me my fade-away jump shot, and she was super. I'm sure we got on her nerves, but she never put her hands on us and she took our verbal abuse and gave it back better. My brothers Ken Jr., aka Man, and my younger brother Kirk, aka Kap, are the best brothers a brother could ask for. We did it all. Man, being the oldest, was the ring leader, taking no prisoners when it came to whatever game we played, and being Jr., I thought that dad showed him more love. Kap, being the baby of the group, got love from everyone. I know mom and pop loved me. It didn't stop me from getting the most spankings, or should I say whippings, but it kept me in line. My Uncle Chuck always looked out for me. He made sure I had some new shoes for every basketball season and he would always let me use his car for the prom. He believed in me and pushed me to be the best. We had a love-hate relationship, and I loved it.

Friends: boy, this list is so big for me. I'm sure I'll speak about my friendships later on in the book, but one of the things that kept me playing basketball at a high level was the competition I received when I would go to the parks and play after school. My Culpepper crew included my boys Frank White, Dino, Jewel, Earl, Chuck, Puff, Matt, Walter, and so many others that helped me maintain playing at a high level. Thank you. I was raised in Culpeper, Virginia, and every Sunday we would go into the side yard and play softball with a plastic ball. This was one of the sports that we all played as a family. I remember learning the game and my dad teaching us early about teamwork. I guess you could say I was a poor sport, but what's wrong with trying to win all of the time every time we played? I was happy when I won, sad and mad when I lost. I was so serious about basketball that if someone blocked my shot I cried, but I learned not to get my shot blocked.

When we were kids we made baskets out of plastic race car tracks. We'd take the track and make it into a rim, then cut newspapers into little strips and tape them on the track to make nets. The rim started off low, but the older we got the more nails we would see in the walls until dad decided it was time to go outside. We loved being outside anyway. It didn't matter; we just nailed them into the trees and took it from there. Finally we got our own rim and I tell you, the game took off. We played one-on-one, two-on-two, whatever or whoever was willing to play, we played. Our house would be so crowded and we played all day and all night. Our parents never had to worry about us, they could just look out the window and know it was all good. I remember playing by myself and always taking and making the game winning shot, and if I missed, you know I got fouled and had to go to the free throw line and make free throws for the win. I did that so many times that when I was faced with those situations; it was like I had already done it. It helped me to become a great free throw shooter and a clutch shot maker.

# Chapter 2
# Brothers

I am really tight with my brothers'. These two affected my life in a way that helped me get to where I was trying to go. As for nicknames, my older brother's nickname is Man, my nickname is Mister and Kirk's nickname is Kap. I got my nickname by singing the song "Mister Big Stuff", an old classic from back in the day. When I was playing little league football for the first year at 7, my dad was ready to leave the park, but I kept playing with my new friends.

He yelled, "Mister Jennings, get your butt over here!"

My friends were like, "He calls you Mister?"

And I said "Yep" and it stuck.

My older brother Man was and is the best big brother a younger brother could ask for. He showed me love but he also made me earn every victory, especially in basketball. He helped provide direction for me in all sports. He led by example: he was shorter than everyone else, but that never seemed to bother him. I couldn't beat him in anything, so I had to dig deeper and hit him where it hurts. I remember stepping thru his drum set he got for Christmas, and stepping on his electric football set. Instead of him whipping my butt, he played the mental game early. He wouldn't talk to me. I would talk to him but he ignored me and sometimes it would last as long as 3 weeks. I stopped breaking his stuff.

My younger brother Kap is the best little brother a brother could ask for. When I started to understand what hard work could do to improve my abilities as a basketball player, it was Kap that worked out with me and never said a word. Whatever I did, he joined me. When I would get up at 6 A.M. in the morning to jog, Kap would jog with me. When I would come back and shoot 200 jump shots before school started, it was Kap that rebounded for me, and when I told him to shoot, he would say "I'm good, it's about you." He's part of the reason I became a great shooter. We played 2-on-2 against all comers and we beat them all. Whoever would team up with Man, we beat them…Cee, Frank, Dino, Rod, Leo, G Funk. It didn't matter, me and Kap found a way to win the series.

All I know is, brothers are special people. We never raised a hand at each other. I take nothing away from my relationship with my sisters. I love them to death but it's something about living your dream and having your family and friends there to share it with you. The Jennings' family are good people. We aim to help and not hurt, and I believe through my upbringing I will make a difference in other peoples' lives. Thank you guys for the love and support and always know that I love you.

# Chapter 3:
# Organized Basketball

I would say that in the 7th grade I knew I wanted to be some type of athlete. My dad was known to call me lazy, and he always said, "You better make it in something, because everyday work isn't for you." My 7th grade year was the first time I got to try out for a basketball team, the Culpeper Cougars. My older brother played for this team and played very well, so I'd been looking forward to this opportunity ever since I finished the 6th grade. In youth basketball I had scored 39 points in a game, with no 3 point line. The next weekend, my good friend Jeff Jorgenson scored 40, and he always reminds me that he had the top single game scoring output every time we mention the old days. I made the Cougars team as a 7th grader and it was a great feeling to know I was finally part of a winning basketball program. I didn't start right away but by the 8th game I was starting. I played for Coach Shinberger. He was a nice coach and he helped me get better. My 8th grade year I would start to play with more confidence because the 9th graders were gone. That year I averaged 17 points and 6 assists. I was really quick, and I was fundamentally sound at this point of my career. I used to steal the ball a lot and I was good at making lay-ups, so I got a lot of my points that way. We only lost one game that year, and I was real excited about the upcoming season.

# Chapter 4:
# Learning How to Shoot

I was getting ready for our 9th grade year. I knew we could go undefeated and I also knew I was going to have a better year, but a strange thing happened. On the first day of try-outs, right before we were going to have our first team meeting, Coach Shinberger called me into his office. I'm telling him how good we're going to be and he stops me in mid-sentence and tells me that the varsity coach wants to talk with me about playing varsity. I was in shock, but I met with Coach Thornhill and he told me he wanted me to play varsity. Coach Thornhill was a former player at Culpeper High School and set many records for the program as a player. He could really shoot the ball. I don't know what he saw in me. My brother Man had just graduated and had a great high school career but he didn't get the chance to play college ball because of his size. I was thinking "He's really good, better than me." If he can't play college basketball, I knew it was going to be tough for me. Coach Thornhill told me he wasn't bringing me up to varsity to sit on the bench; if I worked hard, I'd find playing time. I left his office knowing that the decision was going to be up to me.

I went home and talked with mom and dad. They knew how much I enjoyed playing with my friends, and we were good, but my dad told me if I want to get better I have to play against better players. My mom has always had a strong faith and she told me to believe in myself, because God won't put me through anything I can't handle. Those encouraging words from them made me believe that I could play on the varsity even though I was only 5'5 and 135 pounds. I told Coach I wanted to play varsity and he said, "Welcome to the team." One of the things that bothered me the most was that I knew some of the guys but I didn't know them too well. These guys were older, talking about girls and parties. I felt so out of place but I practiced hard and tried to get better every day.

The season didn't start off like I wanted it to. I didn't play the first 2 games, and we lost those games. You know how I feel about losing, and I couldn't find anything fun to say about the game that I found fun in no matter what. Every time I had a chance, I would go back and watch my boys on the Cougars play and they were playing well. But this one game that I got to watch, they were playing against Warren County. This team was really good. They had this point guard named Cee Russell. He was doing things with the basketball that I hadn't seen anyone do, and on top of that, his team was killing my boys. I was in the bleachers wishing I could play! That day made me realize that I'm not the only one working on the game of basketball. I always said other players are trying to get better, and you better be working on your game because when you meet that person that's working harder than you, it's going to be a tough game. Cee is one of my best friends now, but little did he know that he helped me to become a complete basketball player.

We had 7 more games left in the season and the hard work is beginning to pay off, because I was starting to play more. I remember we had to go on the road and play Caroline and they had already beaten us at our place. I didn't play that game. They were the best team in the district, but this night would be my coming-out party, so to speak. I came in the game and scored my career high of 18 points and had 5 assists. We lost the game but it was my best performance of the season and it made me feel good about myself. We finished the season 5-15 and we were getting ready for our district tournament. We had to go on the road to play James Monroe and they were ready for us, but we played better than I expected. The game was close until the end and that's when it happened: I got fouled with 2 seconds left in the game and we were down 1. I remember this like yesterday, I've put myself in this situation so many times in my driveway and their coach calls a timeout to try to make me nervous. Me, nervous? I don't think so. But while we're in the huddle, Coach tells the team, "After Mister makes these, don't foul," and he looked at me, and that gave me confidence. I went to the foul line, made both free throws, and we won by 1. We lost in the semi-finals to Spotsylvania High School. We had them at half time but they came back to close out our season. We finished 6-16. This record was terrible in my eyes, but the experience I gained from this year would always be with me. I didn't have too many losing seasons in my career. They say you always remember your first.

# Chapter 5:
# Learning How to Score

Looking back at my career, my sophomore year was very important. I was a varsity starter and leader. When I played little league football I was the quarterback, so leading a team wasn't new to me. I was just hoping that we'd have a better season than my freshman year. That is how I approached the season. This year was the year I was introduced to the green light. The green light is what every basketball player that is really good on the offensive end loves to hear. It means you can shoot the ball and not worry about coming out after a bad shot. I didn't want to abuse the privilege so I didn't shoot the ball every time. But, I wasn't afraid to shoot when I was open. I would wake up at 6 A.M. and my younger brother Kirk would join me in my morning jog. We would walk outside and stretch. You could see the dew on the ground. Plenty of mornings when it was foggy, it would be so cool and peaceful. My mom would be driving to work and she would always blow her horn at us with that friendly smile, showing us that she approved of the work we were putting in, just being on our country road made me love the game of basketball even more. I know that jogging in the mornings before school and coming back and shooting 200 jump shots helped me. One thing I figured out about shooting, when you're by yourself you better be able to make shots because when you have a hand in your face while you're shooting, the shot becomes difficult.

I tried to take advantage of all opportunities. We started off winning our first 3 games, beating teams that we were supposed to beat, and when the Battlefield District began, we were ready. I was off to a good start, averaging 18 points. Then it happened: my first injury, back spasms. I didn't know what happened. I reached for a pass and the next thing I know, I'm on the floor. I sat out for two games and thought I was going to die. I hated not being able to play. I find myself telling kids when they're hurt to take their time coming back, because if you come back too early you could do something that could make it worse. I wish I could've told myself that during these times. I was released to come back and play but the coach was very selective with my playing time. I got healthy and picked my game back up. My dad and uncle were in the stands yelling at me to shoot the ball every time. It makes me laugh when I see parents doing that today. Little do they know, they're putting pressure on their kid. When my dad and uncle weren't telling me to shoot it, they were yelling at the referees. It got to the point where they were becoming more of a distraction and I remember telling them, "If you guys are going to yell and scream, I'd prefer you not come to the games." I didn't know what they would say, but thank God they listened. We finished the season 15-6.

We won our district tournament and I was named the tournament's most valuable player. After the championship game I got to cut down the nets with the rest of my teammates, and it was a great feeling. That was another first and something I'll never forget. Our season wasn't finished. We were headed for our first regional tournament, hoping to get a chance to play for a state title. Boys basketball in Culpeper, Virginia is very important. We only had one state title at Culpeper County High School and that was back in 1972. Watching the older guys ahead of me made me want to add a state title with one of my teams that I played with. Our first round regional opponent was Warren County. We didn't know much about them. We were excited to be playing, and this was new to all of us. We beat them with solid defense and timely shooting.

Our next opponent was Robert E. Lee. They were the number 1 team in the state and they had a player named Kevin Madden. He was a senior and had signed a letter of intent to go to North Carolina. The game was at their place and it was packed. We didn't care, we were happy to be playing in the regional semifinals. We got Kevin into early foul trouble and took an early lead, but then one of their sophomores, Todd Dunnings, stepped up and made the game interesting. Kevin came back into the game but he fouled out and we really felt good about our chances. We were up 1 with 12 seconds left and Todd made a big play for them. We had a chance for the game winner but failed, and that's where our season ended. I didn't play too well offensively, only 8 points. I remember being in the locker room after the game. One teammate started crying then another and another until pretty soon we were all hugging each other talking about how next year was going to be different. Our final record was 19-7 and I ended up making 1st team All Region and 1st team all Battlefield District.

# Chapter 6:
# Learning How to Play

Talk about being excited for my third basketball season! We had all of our main players returning: Freddie, Anthony, Steve, Garland, Kelly, Chuck, Earl, Donald, Jonathon, Coy, and Bradley. This team was probably the best team I played on at the time. We all tried to do what we could to win. I was the ring leader and at this point the love for the game of basketball was in me. I stopped playing football, and I really loved football, but getting hurt in 4 of the 10 games made my dad tell me to concentrate on basketball and baseball. I did what I was told and found myself on the basketball court every day. We got off to a great start winning our first 8 games. It was great to play on a team where we put winning first.

One of the games that proved to me that we were a team was the home game against Spotsylvania. They were our rivals and we knew since we beat them in the conference championship, they were out for revenge. The night before the game, my mom (who is the best cook ever), Kap, and I woke up feeling awful. Kap was throwing up, I was throwing up, and mom wasn't feeling the best either. She had to go to work, and we had our big game against Spotsy. Well, somehow mom got us in the car and got us to the doctor. I told him, "I have to be to school before lunch because we have a huge game tonight", and he told me I shouldn't play. He knew I wasn't going to sit out this game, so he gave us some medicine, and I got to school by lunch.

My teammate Freddie said, "I didn't think you were coming today."

I told him I was sick and planned on playing but didn't know for sure, it would be a game-time decision.

He told me not to worry, "I got your back" and Freddie played his best game of the season.

The gym was packed once again and I saw Freddie do things that I still remember like it was yesterday. His stats for the game were 25 points, 14 rebounds, and 8 assists. I finished with 13 points and got all of those in the 3rd quarter. We beat Spotsy that night and finished the season as regular season champions. Now we were getting ready for the district tournament. We won that for the second year in a row, I was named 1st team All-Conference and the tournament's MVP for the second straight year.

We were headed back to the regional tournament and we knew what to expect this year. We almost beat the number 1 team in the state last year so our confidence was up. We had to play Waynesboro in the first round, and just like the year before, we won again. The good thing about the tournament was that we hosted it, so we had a slight home court advantage. The gym was packed and I got off to a good start. We coasted to an easy victory. I finished with 18 points and nothing could be better than to have a rematch with the team that finished our season off for us last year, Robert E. Lee. I got my wish because R. E. Lee beat up on their first round opponent pretty good. Now it was our chance to knock them off. We were hyped and we got some new Nike's for the game, blue and gold, just like our uniforms. Payback was definitely on my mind, or should I say *our* minds. Be careful what you ask for! The thing I remember most about the beatdown we took was the tenacious defense they put on us, and especially on me. I was double-teamed all night and didn't make the open shots that I did take. To make a long story short, they beat us by 20 points and they held me to

7 points once again. The main thing I realized was that our seniors were done, none of them had any opportunities to play college basketball. I was still in the dark about what to do after I graduated, which was now only a year away.

One of my greatest memories of that season was the attention I was getting as a player. I was named 1st team All Region again, and 2 days later, while I was hanging out with my brother Man, I received a phone call from our area newspaper sports writer. He called and asked me what I thought about being 1st team All State? I nearly dropped the phone! The next thing I know, my brother and his friends are looking at me, and when I hung the phone up he asked, "What was that about?" and I told him that I made the All-State 1st team. You would've thought we just won some type of championship; they were laughing and picking me up. I was thinking they were happier than me, but the tears in my eyes showed that they couldn't be as happy as I was. I went home excited to tell my mom and dad what happened. I busted into the house and saw them sitting down watching television and I was excited.

They looked at me and I said "Guess what!"

And they were like "What?"

I told them I was 1st team All State, and they went back to watching television. I went from cloud nine to cloud zero.

I remember saying, "I was just with people that weren't family that are happier than you guys!"

Now that I think about it, I overreacted. All the things that they had to do to make sure that we kept a roof over our heads, food in our mouths and love in our hearts… that was enough. I know my parents love me and I realized what's special to me might not be as special to anyone else. We finished the season 22-4. My accomplishments were Central Virginia Player of the Year, 1st team All District, 1st team All Region, and 1st team All State.

# Chapter 7:
# Have Fun.

My senior year was a special year for me. First of all, I knew what kind of year I needed to have if I wanted to play college basketball, because I was an All-State performer and no one was sending me any letters to go to college. I never discussed with any of the former seniors what to expect your senior year, so I learned by trial and error and I'm glad I didn't make too many errors. You live and you learn, that's what I live by. With my girlfriend heading off to college, I was starting to find out things for myself. One realization I had was that the guys that I played with that were seniors were back supporting us at our games now. I felt like they had enough talent to play at one of the college levels, but they didn't get the proper help. So my senior year was on and poppin'! I knew what we had accomplished as a team and what I did as an individual. I worked really hard on the basketball court and did enough to get by in the classroom. This team wasn't as talented as the previous team, but this was my crew, the guys I played with when we were younger. My boy Chuck was the point guard. He was my best friend, and still is. My boy Earl stepped up and so did the rest of the team.

Back in the 9th grade if you recall, I talked about another point guard named Cee Russell. He totally dominated our 9th grade team and I watched it first-hand. I walked into Coach T's office and asked him about our schedule, and he told me we would be playing Warren County. Come to find out this was Cee's senior year too. I was finally going to play against the guy that I thought was outstanding. I remember it like yesterday. We had to play them at our place first and it was packed once again. I was at the gym early and I saw him walk in. I was thinking he doesn't know about me but I know about him. Come to find out later, he had listened to some of our games on the radio and he was familiar with me. When we walked out before the tip off and shook hands, I could tell by his look that he was ready. The first shot I took was from 22 feet and it was all net. It would've been a 3 pointer but we didn't have a 3 point line back then. We ended up winning that game. I finished with 26 points, Cee had 21 points. Three weeks later we played them at their place and they returned the favor beating us. Cee ended up attending Slippery Rock University where he is still the all-time assist and steals leader. We're best of friends today and laugh about that game often.

The Battlefield district was getting better, and anytime you win the title 2 straight years, you have to know that everyone, and I mean everyone wants to beat you. Orange County was one of those teams. They were up and coming, and they had two big young guys that turned out to be very good basketball players. One of them was Matt Burrell. He was a bruiser, 6'6", 230 pound sophomore. I didn't think they would be ready to play against us, but by the end of the season, they were ready for everyone. I'm not much of a trash talker but I remember before we beat Orange at our place, the crowd was going crazy and Matt looked like he was a little nervous. I told him "Don't get scared now, it's too late. Just take this butt-kicking like a young man." He's one of my best friends now and with me being 5'7" and he's 6'7", we laugh about it.

During my senior year I started to notice different men coming to our practices and our games. I was being recruited by Emory and Henry, a Division 3 school. The coach would watch me practice and I was excited by that, but then another man showed up for one of our games. He was dressed to impress.

I mean Culpeper is a small town, so any new faces stood out. Well it turns out that this new face belongs to Dave Hanners, an assistant for East Tennessee State University, and that night I didn't disappoint him. I had 35 points in a win over King George. Coach Hanners introduced himself to me after the game and told me about ETSU. I looked them up in the sporting news and saw they were coming off a bad year. Their record was 7-21 and they didn't have any returning point guards. A week later the top assistant at ETSU, Alan LeForce, came to one of my games and from a fan standpoint, he picked a good night. That night I was closing in on being the all-time leading scorer in the Battlefield District. I had already broken Coach Thornhill's records and was moving closer to the district mark.

Coach L. got to the game early and he didn't want to drive 5 ½ hours to see a 5'7" point guard that no one was recruiting, but he knew my cousin and did it as a favor to her. Thanks TT! Well he gets to the game and acts like he's an insurance salesman just out enjoying high school basketball. He asks one of the fans if we have any good players and they told him about me. I'm shooting deep shots and he's thinking that I must be a little cocky, but I call it being a showman, smile…. Anyway, the game gets started, and I'm 16 points from breaking the record, and every time I score, the student body is putting signs up that say "Mister needs 14 points", then when I score again, "Mister needs 12 points," all the way down to when I break the record. When the referees stop the game, my family and friends rush the court and my teammates lift me up, and we're still in the 3$^{rd}$ quarter! They take me to where my mom is sitting and she's so happy for me, she's crying, and that makes me cry. Then after everything settles down, I shake the hands of the opposing team and resume the game, which we win. That was a special moment in my basketball career.

We're number 1 heading into the district tournament and we win our first 2 rounds and face Orange County in the finals. We're the defending champs and we lost the game by 2 points. Even though that was a tough loss, especially after winning the last 2 tournaments, we still had to get ready for the regional tournament. One thing about my senior year, we all understood that this might be the last time we play with each other so let's go out with a bang. We played Osbourn in the first round, and since they were hosting the tournament it wasn't that bad of a drive for us, only 40 minutes. We played in their building earlier in the season and won a Christmas tournament so we were ready.

We won our first round game, and you know who else won their first round game? You guessed it, Robert E. Lee! I was so sick of this team I couldn't stand it. I mean, they beat me as a sophomore, and they really stuck it to us my junior year, and now we get to face them for the 3$^{rd}$ straight time in the regional semi-finals. There's this saying, "3$^{rd}$ time's the charm", or "It's always hard to beat a team 3 times", and I didn't want to lose to this team 3 years in a row. To make things personal, they held me to 7 points each game, and I was not going to let that happen this time. Well, we didn't get off to a good start and we were down 19 at the half. Everything was going their way and we just couldn't get going. At halftime I could see it in our faces. We didn't think we were going to win, but I told them, "We got to keep playing hard. I'm not going to give up! Y'all can do what you want, but I'm not giving up!"

We cut into the lead a little and at the start of the 4$^{th}$ quarter we were still down 13 points. I remember right before the 4$^{th}$ period started and we came out of the huddle, I pulled the other 4 players together and looked them dead in their eyes and told them, "Don't give up on me." I went off for 12 straight points and the game was tight at the end. We were down 1 point with 20 seconds left. I got a steal and pushed the ball up the court. The defense got to me so I passed it to one of my teammates and he missed the layup. They got the rebound and we had to foul. They made their free throws and we lost by 3. So R. E. Lee knocked me out of the regional tournament 3 straight years. I finished with 29 points in my last high school game and I never got the opportunity to play in a state tournament and win a state title. We finished that season 19-7 and

I was 1$^{st}$ team All District, 1$^{st}$ team All Region, 2$^{nd}$ time Central Virginia Player of the Year, 1$^{st}$ team All State for the second year and I was the all-time leading scorer at Culpeper High School. I was also the all time leading scorer in the Battlefield District with 1,740 points. I believe records are made to be broken, and I would love to be there when someone breaks my records.

# Chapter 8:
# Recruitment and Decisions

After my senior season, I was thankful for everything we accomplished as a team and what I accomplished as a player. I never played the game to be rewarded; I played the game to be respected. Looking back on it, just dreaming to do something great with my life was taking place. I can remember writing my signature a certain way just in case someone asked me for my autograph and after one of my games as a sophomore it happened! A little kid came up to me and asked me for my autograph. I thought one of my boys put him up to it, and I asked the kid that. He said no one put him up to it. He said, "I like the way you play and I think you're good."

ETSU invited me in for my first official visit and it was the first time I'd ever been on a plane. I remember looking out of the window and seeing my mom, dad, and nanny waving at me, and it hit me that I might be leaving home and it was time to grow up. I arrived and Coach Hanners showed me around campus. Then Chad Keller took me out to eat and introduced me to some of the players. During my visit, we had another guard visiting at the same time. His name was Alvin West. He was from North Carolina and I could tell this wasn't his first time visiting a school. He asked me what position I played, and I told him point guard. He told me he played the point guard and shooting guard, so the friendly competition began in my mind right there. He asked me, "If they offer you a scholarship, what are you going to do?" I told him I would accept if they offered. I got to meet Coach Robinson, and he turned out to be a super nice man. I knew I would enjoy playing for him, but he didn't mention anything about a scholarship. When my visit was over, I had one last breakfast with Coach Robinson before going home, and he offered me a full scholarship. Inside I was so happy, but on the outside I played it cool and asked him if he minded if I went home and talked it over with my family. He said it would be no problem. When I got home the talk went like this in the car… "I had a great visit. They want me to come here. I'll be on a full scholarship and I'm taking it." Mom and Dad were happy and I called Coach Robinson and let him know I would be attending ETSU.

# Chapter 9:
# Beginning the Dream

I was off to college, and what an experience this was. I remember when my girlfriend left to go to college the year before, along with my basketball partners and friends, I was shaken but being with my family made it easier to deal with. Now I was off to college. ETSU is only 5 ½ hours from Culpeper, VA, so the trip wasn't that bad. You would think that getting away from your family wouldn't be so hard. Boy was I wrong! After my mom, dad, Trina (girlfriend), Kap, Eric, Sandy, Carl, and Uncle Chuck dropped me off, I sat in my room teary-eyed and stomach hurting, wondering if I made the right decision. I hadn't met all of my new teammates, so I was lying on my bed and an upperclassman named Rodney Jones came by my room. He could tell I was sad and the destruction that I caused in the bathroom made him close the door right away. He said "What's up freshman?"

And I thought, here we go with the freshman stuff!

I said "What's up?"

And he asked me my name.

Well my nickname is all I've been going by, so I said "Mister"

And he said "Mister what?"

I said "That's my nickname."

He said "What's your real name? I'm not calling you Mister."

I said "Keith."

He said, "Let's go Keith, I'll show you around campus."

I was happy that Rodney came by. This would be something I would do for all new guys if they needed it, MEMORIES. I met the rest of the guys at our first team meeting, and then after that I got to know the other freshmen. I already knew Alvin. I met Major Geer who could play the point guard and shooting guard. He was real quiet and low key, but he was explosive and he could shoot the ball really well. Greg Dennis was our big guy. I had never played with a big man that could do it all. Greg could post up, he could make the 3 pointer, he could play one-on-one, and he would dunk on you as well as look at you. I knew he would be on the receiving end of a lot of my assists. Mike Woods was a do-it-all type of player, and he would make me a better player.

We all went to Brooks Gym and played. Just watching these guys play, and playing with them, I was smiling ear to ear, because these guys played hard, and that's how I always played the game too. I knew we didn't have any returning point guards, so I was ready to fight for that position. Battling with Alvin and Major every day wasn't easy, but being a shooting guard in high school really helped me. They didn't know I could shoot the ball, and I was more than happy to show them. When we first met with our other teammates and played 5 on 5, they were trying to pick up teams.

I said, "We'll play you guys." I wanted to take care of that freshman nonsense real early.

They were like, "Okay freshmen, we'll break you all in." Boy, did we surprise them! We didn't lose. Right then I knew some of us would be starting the season in the starting lineup and 3 of us were. I found out that our coaches wanted good things for us. Coach Hanners was the best. He made cookies and told us stories about playing for Dean Smith at UNC. All the coaches were extremely helpful, and being away from our families made my ETSU family even stronger. Coach Howat was great, Coach Radabau was great, Coach Lebo was cool, Coach Peterson was great, and Coach Shulman was the man. All of these guys would impact my life in a positive way. Coach Young and Coach LeForce were the guys that talked about discipline and defense all the time, and Coach Robinson was definitely a great guy to play for and a great guy to talk to. Thank you coaches, I only hope I can impact a student athlete's life like you did for me.

There is one special coach that helped me, and he had nothing to do with putting me into the game. That was our strength and conditioning Coach Lee Marrow. Whoever came up with the phrase "tough guy" had to be thinking about Coach Marrow. He made us all tougher, faster, stronger, and even more important mentality tough. He was a treat to be around, even when he was running us like crazy. I remember when we got settled and were getting ready for our first weight room workout. First of all, I was never a serious weight lifter. I did push-ups and sit-ups and my dad gave us the old school weights that were plastic with the sand in them, but unless I was doing squats I didn't touch them.

So   we were off to the weight room. I never let another player intimidate me, but when I saw those big 45 pound plates on that bar resting over the bench, I was thinking, "I know I can't lift that!" The upper classmen were laughing and I bet it was because they probably felt the same way as freshmen. Coach Marrow told us not to worry, that we'll get stronger and I went from not being able to lift 120 pounds to maxing out by the time I was a senior at 275 pounds. That was the weight lifting part, the conditioning part was a whole different level. I remember Coach Marrow wore this green t-shirt with a skull on it, and it had a knife between the eyes. There was no use in asking him what we were doing that day because that shirt said it all. We were going to run a lot. Basketball is just that. You have to prepare yourself to run. It's a constantly moving game. Very seldom are you standing still. Maybe when someone is shooting free throws or maybe when you're on the bench, but you have to be able to run. I didn't mind that. I just didn't like running on the track. I prefer the court. I jogged a lot but this type of conditioning had me in great shape. Some of the other guys didn't want to play after we ran, but I wanted to play, and found myself with the other freshmen playing and working on our game while the upper classmen just went off in their own direction.

I want to talk about the point guard position. Like I said, I was the shooting guard in high school, but I knew that I would be a point guard in college. I didn't have a problem with that. I would call myself unselfish, so passing the ball was easy for me. I knew as a point guard I had to be a leader. I had to understand what the coach wanted from me and I had to figure out what my teammates could and couldn't do. I had to be a pest on defense and I had to be ready to score when the opportunity presented itself. I did all of these things as a freshman. I was one of the players that understood my position early at ETSU. ETSU didn't have any returning point guards so the opportunity to play that position was presented to me as a freshman. Alvin and Major could also play the point guard, but we all worked each other really hard and we made each other better. Passing is what I like to do the most. For any point guard, in my personal opinion, that wants to shoot first and pass second, you're not a point guard. I wish these so-called coaches and media people would stop calling these guys point guards. Point guards don't shoot the ball 25 times a game or even 20 times unless your teammates are fouling out. Point guards run the show and if you want your team to be successful, they better run the show right.

Our first game was against UNC Greensboro. I was nervous my first college game but it was against a Division 3 team and we're Division 1, so I thought we would beat them. I learned at an early stage in my career, anyone can win on any night. We lost our first game and lost it by 25 points. We never got the chance to redeem ourselves against them. They were so lucky, because anyone that beat us, if we played them again, the outcome was usually in our favor. Our freshman year was filled with more downs than ups. My roommate was a guy named Sidney Primus. He was a long, 6'7" small forward, but he had an injury prone season due to a separated shoulder. He missed a lot of the season. We got along pretty good as roommates but he left before the year was finished, and the year before the team only won 7 games and lost 21. We were definitely the new kids on the block and the block was hot.

I remember playing South Eastern Conference power, Mississippi State University. They were good and they beat us pretty bad, and while doing so, they talked a lot of trash. They would say things like, "Welcome to the SEC," and, "You guys are terrible," and, "Where's East Tennessee?" We would remember all of that. On the drive back to Johnson City, we were definitely acting like freshmen. We were laughing and cracking jokes on each other. I remember Coach Hanners coming back to us and saying, "Guys, after losing like that, I wouldn't be back here laughing and joking." He never had to give us that talk again. When he finished talking, we were quiet for 10 minutes and started cracking jokes again… FRESHMEN! Coach Robinson was thinking differently. After the long 15 hour bus ride back home, we were getting off the bus and thinking what would we do with this day off when Coach Robinson told us to get changed into our practice gear. We practiced for 2 hard hours and that was the last time he had to do that. We got better as the season went along. Playing college basketball as a freshman was fun. The only thing I didn't like was the losing. I hated it. I go into every game thinking I'm going to win, and that attitude just wasn't here at ETSU when we arrived. We finished the regular season 14-15. We were getting ready for our first southern conference tournament and I was excited. We got matched up with Appalachian State in the first round. They had beaten us both games during the regular season. Well, like I said in high school, it's always tougher to beat a team 3 times. We beat Appy State 82- 73. When the media picks you to lose and you win, it's a great feeling. In the next round we had to play Virginia Military Institute. They were tough during the year but we beat them both times. This time would be a tough 3$^{rd}$ time for us, and they took advantage of us. Their twins, Ramon and Damon Williams put on a show and they sent us home. I made the All-Freshman team that year, and knew next year would be different.

# Chapter 10:
# Playing as a team.

Experience is the key if you want to continue to get better at what you love or like to do. I took what I learned as a freshman and since I was a year older, I tried not to make the same freshman mistakes again. Our freshman class, now sophomores, made a pact to keep working hard in the off season even if it meant not doing things that you would like to do. I really felt like I dedicated myself to be the best basketball player possible while I was at ETSU. This was the year I could see things were starting to change. Nothing against the seniors that graduated, but I believe they were used to losing and didn't give us the senior leadership we needed. They were good guys though.

One of our biggest surprises was the media people picked us to win the conference. Coach Robinson thought that put too much pressure on us, and at the time we didn't know what came with being number one in the conference. Our second year together started off with a transfer from the Clemson University football team. His name was Marty Story. He was 6'3", 200 pounds. The fact that he played football showed me he was tough, and we turned out to be roommates. Marty was from Greenville, Tennessee. He was on a football scholarship to Clemson, but one day the head coach said some things that made Marty want to play basketball instead. I'm glad he made that decision. Our first conversation was about me throwing the alley-oop and him catching it. We worked that out real quick. We were roommates the next two years. He was a great roommate and his family was real nice.

The seniors, Rodney Jones, Mark Larkey, Lavelle Webster, and Steve Cox helped us continue to get better. They helped me understand what being a senior meant. I know they all wanted to play more, but Coach Robinson decided to go with young guys as freshmen and it didn't change our sophomore year. Confidence was the key for me this year. I always believed in my God-given ability, but for some reason I felt the game started coming easy to me. It seemed we all were hungry and had something to prove. We also had 2 freshmen that joined our team, James Jacobs and Calvin Talford. These two guys would make practice better right from the start. Like when we were freshmen, we knew that if we gave them some direction they would be just fine. Calvin was an impact freshman, which means he played right away. He was a great athlete. He was All State in 4 different sports in high school and was recently inducted in the Virginia High School Hall of Fame. I didn't see too many dunks in high school, but Calvin had a dunk highlight tape that was the most incredible dunk footage I witnessed for a high school player. I remember we had to choose what number we wanted when we arrived at college. I wore #20 in high school, but Rodney Jones wore #20 and wasn't about to give it to me, so I settled for #22. When Calvin arrived, they asked him what number he wanted and he told our equipment guy he wanted #22. The guy said, "Sorry, that's Mister's number," and Calvin settled for #24. The things we got to see everyday in practice were jaw-dropping. I wish the fans could've seen some of the things they missed. Needless to say, there was a new dunk king in Johnson City and his name was Calvin Talford.

We got off to a good start, winning our preseason games and starting off 2-0. Then we got our first taste of the big time. We got invited to the Carrier Classic in Syracuse, New York and our first round opponent was Syracuse. They had Derrick Coleman, Sherman Douglas, Billy Owens and Steve Thompson and they were nationally ranked. This was a big challenge for us, walking into their dome and seeing all that orange. They beat us by 39 points. I played okay against Sherman. I finished with 21 points and 10 assists. After that game I really believed I could play against the top point guards in the country, and Sherman was a projected first round pick in the upcoming NBA draft. Sherman Douglas finished his college career as the all-time assist leader in NCAA history.

We came back the next night and beat Miami of Ohio. Alvin blocked their shooting guard's shot in the final seconds to secure the win. The final score was 79-78. We came back home to play Mississippi State at our place. If you remember they beat us as freshmen by 27 points, so we were looking forward to this game. We got our revenge and beat them 91-82. Just like they told us, we told them, "Welcome to the Southern Conference!" It was funny to me because Alvin was our major trash talker, and when MSU beat us, they were talking a lot. When the game was all but done, their coach didn't like the way Alvin was talking. I told him, "We didn't like the way your team was talking last season!" I love payback, especially when I'm the payer.

I remember we had a tournament in California and Coach R. had some personal affairs he had to take care of, so Coach LeForce took over for us. He was real nervous and even though he was 2-0 after that weekend, he lost more hair and he didn't have that much to begin with. One of the games that really stood out for me, was playing Wake Forest University. I went home the weekend before this game, and when I went home I always took advantage of playing with my friends from home. During this time, I sprained my ankle. I didn't know what I was going to do but I talked to one of the coaches and he smoothed it over with Coach Robinson. I ended up playing but I didn't start for the first time since my freshman year started. The coaches decided to start Calvin. He was coming off the bench, but he told the guys he's not coming off the bench anymore. When I came back the following week, he was in the starting lineup and stayed there. After that game we got a little big-headed and lost 3 games in a row, and I'm glad to say a 3-game losing streak was the most we ever had while we were at ETSU. We never had 4 losses in a row. I remember right before the tournament, all the guys were in the cafeteria eating dinner and it was crowded. I was coming back to the table with my food and I put my food on the table. I didn't notice Calvin being quiet. As soon as I go to sit down, Calvin pulls my chair from under me. I'm on my back with my legs up in the air and everyone is laughing. By the time I got up, Calvin was half way down the hallway. I didn't pass the ball to him for 2 weeks! It was funny though.

# Chapter 11:
# Taste of the Big Time

The regular season ended and we finished 4$^{th}$ in the conference and had to play the Citadel. They had beaten us two weeks earlier at their place by 3 points, so they had to like their chances on a neutral court. The Citadel had an older player named Patrick Elmore. He was 25 years old (didn't look it) playing against us teenagers, but as I said, we didn't back down from anyone. I grew up going to the park, playing against older men just getting off from work and drinking some cold beers before they came to the park to beat up on us. It made me tougher. This game was going back and forth. We were up and then they would take the lead. We were up 2 points with 25 seconds left in the game and the Citadel had the ball. Their big guy Patrick was killing us and I knew the way things were going, being down 2 points, they would probably get him the ball. When they tried to pass the ball to him, I sneaked up on him from behind, stole the ball, and took it in for a lay-up to close out the game. We won 93-89.

Now we had to play the number one team in the conference, UT-Chattanooga. They had some tough trash-talking players, and the ring leader was Benny Greene. He was a slick talking, dead eye shooter that lead his team in scoring. They beat us both times during the regular season, but you know the saying that it's always hard to beat a team 3 times. Well, we came out ready for this game, and on the opening play, we won the tap. I got control of the ball and

I see Calvin running down the right side of the court. I know he knows I'll throw it to him from anywhere because he's that good of a jumper and I'm that good of a passer. Right when I think it's time, I throw the ball up to the basket and he goes up and dunks it in to give us our first 2 points of the game. I got into early foul trouble so I had to sit on the bench early in the second half. Benny Green hit a shot right in front of our bench and told us we can't guard him and we play like girls. Of course I begged Coach to put me back in the game. Once I'm back we start getting control of the game and the momentum changed big-time when I hit Calvin with a pass on the left wing. Calvin goes to the basket and the big man for UTC is racing to catch up with him. When they both jump, Calvin goes a lot higher than their guy and dunks the ball with such force that we know from the look on their faces it was over for them. We ended up winning the game 76-73 but it didn't stop there. After the game, while we're celebrating this tough victory, one of our female cheerleaders runs up to Benny Green and puts the number 1 sign in his face. He pushes her in her face! I know I don't like losing, and I know he didn't like losing to us, but you have to control your emotions.

We get to play on ESPN for the Southern Conference Tournament Championship and this is the first time I've ever played on national television. The winner of this game automatically gets to play in the NCAA Tournament. The only thing standing in our way was Marshall University. You would've thought that this was their home court, because there was so much green and white in the building. Their fans were passionate about supporting the Thundering Herd. This was like the biggest game of my career. There was so much riding on the line. If you lose your season is over, if you win you go to the Big Dance. My stomach was turning flips. I had diarrhea and the 7 p.m. tip-off was 10 minutes away, but eventually my stomach was okay. I was ready to roll. Marshall had a super sophomore named John Taft, and he could score. We would be battling each other for the next 3 years. What started out as a close game ended up as a blow out, and we beat Marshall 96-73. I made the all-tournament team with Major, Greg, and Alvin.

What I remember the most was climbing up the ladder and cutting down the nets. This reminded me of my sophomore year in high school when we won our district tournament and I got to cut down the nets. The joy that I saw on our seniors faces said it all. I always made sure that somebody brought some scissors when we were getting ready for the conference tournament. After this tournament we would be packing our clothes for 3 days, which is if we planned on being there for the championship game. Unlike our freshman year, we didn't know how to pack our clothes. The celebration was incredible! There were smiles on everyone's faces. We were the preseason pick to win the Southern Conference. We didn't win the regular season, but winning the tournament was great. Now we had to wait and see who we would be playing in the first round of the NCAA tournament, and most likely being a mid-major school we would have to play one of the best teams in the country.

# Chapter 12:
# The Dance

Coach Robinson and his family decided we needed some home cooking and invited all the players out to his house for a nice cookout. After we finished eating, the selection committee was coming on. We piled around his television to find out who we would be playing. Then it came on and the announcer said, "#16 seed East Tennessee State University will play #1 seed University of Oklahoma." Oklahoma was ranked number 1 in the nation most of the year, and they had players that the media was saying would play in the NBA. One of them was point guard Mookie Blaylock, and I had watched him play before. He was very quick and led his team in steals. They had another big guy named Stacey King. He led the team in scoring, averaging 27 points per game. I always believed in the element of surprise. We knew about them, but they didn't know anything about us. I'm sure they hadn't heard of us until that game, and on top of that we got to play them in Nashville, Tennessee.

We had a week of practice to prepare for the Oklahoma game and deal with the media. They were asking us how it felt to be David facing Goliath. For me, I've always had to play against bigger opponents, so this was something I was used to. Even though we were playing some of our best basketball at the end of the season, I thought we would play well and see what happens. Vanderbilt's arena was packed, and the atmosphere was great. Oklahoma was introduced first, and they had a good following. Their fans showed up and they were making a lot of noise. Then they introduced us and our fans were louder than their fans! As I was leading us out I noticed that Oklahoma's team stopped what they were doing and just looked at us. The look they were giving was a look of, "Why are you cheering for them? They're going to get killed!" Right then I was telling my guys, "They don't respect us. What are we going to do about that?" I thought this was the best atmosphere going. We were in the NCAA tournament and we were matched up against the best team in the country! I wasn't nearly as nervous as I was before the Southern Conference tournament. We were so focused and I know we believed we could shock the world. I know I believed we could. Coach Robinson was telling us that no 16th seed had ever beaten a #1 seed and challenged us to be the first.

Well, we responded by out-hustling, out-working and out-playing them. Calvin got us off to a great start and Greg was doing his thing. The next thing I knew, we were up 18 points with 8 minutes to go in the first half. I hid my excitement. I learned to keep a stone face, which meant no matter how things were going, I didn't want my opponent to know I was happy or mad. Oklahoma settled down and cut the lead to 9 by halftime. The Oklahoma team was full of veterans. We knew we could keep competing, we just had to stay focused. I stayed out of foul trouble in the first half, but Mookie didn't. It seemed like the roles had changed in the second half, which is the most important half. Now I'm not saying that the referees were bad, but before I knew it I was on the bench with four fouls. We went from being in the lead to now being behind. It was late in the game and I'm back in. I'm doing my best not to foul out. They make a shot to put them up one. I come down the other way, use Greg for a pick, and hit a shot to put us up by one. They make another shot to go back up one. I get fouled and go to the free-throw line, make both shots to put us back up by one. Then Mookie drives past me to the basket. I know I didn't foul him but I hear a whistle. The referee finds me and calls the foul on me. It was my 5th foul so I fouled out with 1 minute and 21 seconds left in the game. That's how the game ended Oklahoma 72, ETSU 71. Walking off the floor with my 5th foul was the toughest walk I ever made in my college career. I wanted to find the referee and ask him how he could make a call like that. I know I didn't touch him but, if you let every basketball player defend himself, he'll tell you that he didn't foul anyone. That was how our season ended, we finished 20-11.

Once we got a taste of the NCAA tournament, we had to go back. Not only that, you want to win it all. I was first team All-Southern Conference that year, and you can believe I was working harder than ever that summer getting ready for my junior year.

# Chapter 13:
# The Value of Experience

We just won 20 games with a bunch of sophomores, so my thinking coming into my junior year was to win more than 20 games, defend our tournament title and get back to the NCAA tournament. We were coming off our best year. Remembering the looks on the faces of seniors Mark, Rodney, Lavelle, and Steve made me want to get back and help Chad go out the same way. Jerry Pelphrey was a new freshman, and he could really shoot the ball. I wondered if he would be tough enough to play with us. I soon found out he was a tough son of a gun. I felt like I was one of the players that understood the game and everything that came along with it, except in the classroom. I'm glad I didn't take any time off because if you want to be the best, there's no rest.

Looking back on our schedule, it was definitely tougher than the previous year, but my dad always said that if you want to get better, you must play against better people. After an early blowout against Charleston, we finally got a shot at the Big Orange, the University of Tennessee. When I arrived in Johnson City I would hear people talk about UT all the time, mainly their football program and girls' basketball program, but Allan Houston and his dad brought new energy to a program that needed it. We went to UT and they quickly found out 2 things: one, the boys from ETSU can really play, and two, no matter where you sit, you'll hear our fans cheering for the Buccaneers. I remember talking with the guys before the game and I didn't have to say much because all of us knew what was at stake. We believed we were the best team in Tennessee and we wanted to show it. Calvin got us off to a great start like he always did. There was something about the beginning of games for Calvin. If he didn't start the game off with an alley-oop, he would hit a 3-pointer. He was just a fun guy to play with. Greg was working them, I ran the show, and we walked out of that place with an 83-70 victory. Starting off 5-1, another major test presented itself to us and it was North Carolina State. It was a cold and icy night at their place and some of my family members drove all the way from Virginia to watch that game. I remember it was Uncle Chuck, Kirk, Dino, and Eric. I told you basketball ran deep in my neck of the woods. NC State had a familiar face with them. Chris Corchiani was a top point guard in the Atlantic Coast Conference and we attended the University of Virginia's basketball camp as seniors in high school. The media was talking real good about him, and my thinking was, if they're talking about him and I play well against him, maybe they'll talk about me. We really surprised them, we came out smoking and we were up 26 with 7 minutes to go before the first half ended. At halftime we were up 14. Coach Robinson used to play at NC State, so we knew this game meant a lot to him. They must have thought that we would fold, but we maintained our lead and ended up winning the game 92-82. I guess you could call it an upset, but we thought we were the better team, or the better prepared team. You see when you play against the so-called "giants," the media really doesn't give you a chance to win. If you do win, it's not because of what you did, it's because the other team didn't do something. I'm just glad they didn't score more points than us, and plus Coach Valvano, rest in peace, said they were preparing for exams and they overlooked us. Hopefully that was a lesson learned.

Then we got on a plane and headed to Hawaii to play in the Chaminade Basketball Tournament. This was a great trip considering I'd never been there before. We had a great time and we finished in 3$^{rd}$ place. The fun part after we finished the tournament was while we were there, one of our classmates, his nickname was "Spanish", told us he would look out for us while we were there. The coaches gave us a day off and we toured the island on mopeds. If you haven't seen what a 6'11" guy and a 6'8" guy looks on mopeds, just ask Greg and Chad. I remember riding my moped and here comes crazy Calvin. Now he's been riding mopeds a lot longer than me, and he would drive close to me like he was going to wreck me. I'm glad he stopped. If you haven't guessed, CT is the jokester of the team. Big Chad was coming over a hill. He zoomed right past me and Marty. When we came over the hill we saw Chad limping, pushing his moped, and hopping on one foot. His knee was bloody, and after we checked on him to make sure he was okay, Marty and I drove off. When we stopped at the light, Marty started laughing so hard we began to cry! We thought it was the funniest thing.

So after we left Hawaii, we stopped back through Los Angeles, California to play UCLA. We thought we would be ready for this game. It was nice going into their building knowing all the tradition they've had, winning so many national titles, and having guys that won the player of the year award. I was hyped and looking forward to the game. We would learn later that Coach Harrick said we had the Hawaii blues, which meant other teams that stopped in to play them after the Hawaii trip didn't play too well, and ETSU would be added to that list. UCLA treated us real bad and beat us even worse, 115-66. That wasn't a fun trip home, to get waxed by 49 points. I'd never been beaten by that much. We woke up after that game and played solid the rest of the season. We only lost 3 more regular season games by a total of 8 points. Wake Forest beat us 73-69, VMI beat us 78-77, and Furman beat us 100-97 in overtime. We won our last 4 games and headed into the conference tournament as the number 1 seed. We didn't lose a single game at home this season. Now that's a home court advantage.

I made sure that when we left Johnson City heading over to Asheville, I told everyone to pack for 3 days and don't forget to bring some scissors. We played Western Carolina in the first round and beat them by 15 points. That set up a game with VMI. Once again it was time to face the twins, Ramon and Damon. In my personal opinion, if it wasn't for our 3-headed guard monster, the twins would've been the best guards in the conference. This game was an ESPN Classic before they started putting out ESPN Classics. VMI had the lead at half time. Not that we were overlooking them, but they played some of the best basketball I had ever seen them play, so we had to fight back. Before you know it we're up 1 late in the game and Alvin slips. One of the twins gets the ball and races to the basket. Being the competitor that Alvin is, he hustled back to make the layup difficult and he did. The twin missed the layup and I got the rebound. They fouled me and I hit both free throws to put us up 3. They had one more shot and missed and Alvin sealed the victory for us. We won 99-94.

Once again we're in the Southern Conference Tournament Championship and once again the game is being played on ESPN. I was starting to get used to this. We had to face another one of our rivals, Appalachian State University.

I believe we were the only team that every team in the conference called a rival. Marshall, UTC, ASU and Furman were rivals to us. ASU was ready for this game and we both knew that winning this game would put us in the big dance. It's like once you taste success, you want it again. We blew ASU out. They played hard, but once we got control of the game we were learning how to close teams out. We did so in a great way. I was voted the tournament's MVP, and when they called my name out it was a great feeling. It amazes me how in this team sport of basketball, they pick one guy out of the 20 that played that night and say he was the best. They should have 3 MVPs. Alvin, Greg, and Major all made the all-tournament team, and of course I brought the scissors to start the net cutting.

It's nice to share the victory with the fans, and I remember climbing up that ladder. While cutting down the nets, I decided to cut a piece of the net and throw it into the sea of fans. Our fans went after that net like it was a winning lottery ticket. I really enjoyed that moment, and it made me realize how special our fans were. On the way home after the game, it was like a convoy. Police officers had their lights on and flashing. It was a wonderful thing to see. When we got back, the fans were there again, congratulating us and making us feel real special. Our record was 27-6 and now we were getting ready to see who we'd have to play in the big dance.

Coach Robinson invited us to his home. After we eat, we were waiting to see who and where we'd be playing this time. Then it comes up, ETSU vs. Georgia Tech in Knoxville, Tennessee. I was excited to be playing so close, and we played UT earlier in the season and beat them. Georgia Tech had All-Americans, Dennis Scott and point guard Kenny Anderson. I was getting another chance to play against one of the top point guards and I couldn't wait. Our main concern was Dennis Scott. He was from Virginia and he was 6'8", 240 pounds. Kenny Anderson was a stand out when he was in the 7th grade. The NBA was waiting for both of these guys. They also had a guy named Brian Oliver that made this team even more dangerous. We thought we could run with anyone, but they seemed to outrun us. We didn't have an answer for Dennis Scott. He finished with 36 points, making shots from everywhere. He even dunked on me, but I didn't jump...smile. I had a better second half. I finished with 17 points, making 5 three-pointers and 10 assists.

My confidence was getting higher and I felt that playing against another top point guard, I held my own. I also helped lead our team to another NCAA tournament appearance. We finished the season 27-7, the most wins in ETSU history. I hope the seniors were happy with their last season. It was great playing with Chad and getting to know his family. Thanks for the love.

# Chapter 14:
# The Value of Experience and Higher Expectations

I remember thinking back in high school my senior year, "This could be my last year of basketball." Then ETSU offered me a full scholarship. Well, now it's my senior year in college and I'm thinking again that this could be my last year of basketball. I knew I wanted a chance to at least see if I could play in the NBA. I felt like I had to go all out and see if that would be possible. During my freshman year, we had lost by 27 to Mississippi State. Then our sophomore year, we lost by 39 to Syracuse and our junior year we lost by 49 to UCLA. I would be heated if anyone beat us by more than 49 our senior year. I just didn't see it happening, but this was our toughest schedule. I remember the seniors were taking pictures everywhere. I especially liked the ones in tuxedos and sporting our championship rings that we had earned the previous two years.

There were some big changes our senior year. First, the coaching change. Les Robinson did the unthinkable to us. We never dreamed that he would leave us our senior year. Since we beat NC State and they had a coaching vacancy, naturally they went after one of their own. Les took the job and I respect him for that. I would love to coach at ETSU one day. I'll be patient and wait for my opportunity. I might've went with him if he would've asked me to, but he already had a stellar point guard in Chris Corchiani, so I wasn't going anywhere. I was very forward about the coaching change. I talked with the guys and told them, "I don't know who they will bring in, but I'd hate for it to be some guy that would come and change the way we play." We were having success and with everyone returning I thought this would be our year to do some serious damage.

After speaking with my fellow seniors, we had a meeting with the president of the University and told him our concerns about a new coach. We told him we would like Coach LeForce to be the new head coach, he knows all of us, and we all respect him. Coach LeForce was announced as the new head coach and we were happy. Coach LeForce was a defensive minded coach. He wanted to shut you down and get after you, and I never had any doubts in his ability to lead us to where we wanted to go. Coach Robinson was a player's coach, which made him smart. He saw what we were developing into and let us play. When Coach Robinson left, he took Assistant Coach Buzz Peterson with him. Buzz was a cool assistant and one of my favorites, but that made room for Coach Shulman. He joined us and, for a tennis player, he was sharp about the game of basketball. He turned out to be my favorite guy to speak with when I had any questions about life, especially women. Coach Lebo helped us a lot and taught us some things that he learned from legendary coach Dean Smith.

We had two new players join our team. They were junior college transfer Rodney English, and freshman Trazel Silvers. These two would help us in a major way. Rodney was a high-flyer. He was only 6'4" but he could jump with the best of them. It didn't start out that way. When he arrived on campus, he was sick, so he didn't get to work out with us the first week. When he came back the coaches had been telling me that he can jump like Calvin. I just couldn't wait to see that, so the first time we got to play together, I threw him an alley-oop. I didn't even throw it too high, and he couldn't catch it. I decided that if he couldn't do any better than what he was showing, there's no way he could play. Of course Calvin told him this and he told me to wait until he felt better. I was like, "Okay, whatever," but sure enough, when he got better, he was one of my favorite guys to play with. I really liked his toughness, he didn't back down against anyone.

Trazel was my new roommate. They said Marty and I were having too much fun so they gave me the freshman. Trazel is 6'7" and he arrived to our room to check in before I did. Davis apartments were small. Since I was the senior, I always stayed on the back side of the room. I did it with Marty for two years, and it wasn't about to change. Well, the highly touted freshman decided he was going to take the back side of the room and put my stuff on the inside. When I got back I kindly moved everything back to the way it was, and I told Trazel, "You're a freshman, you have to wait your turn." We laugh about that today.

We also had a guy that was trying to be a walk-on for our team, and his name was Loren Riddick. It wasn't easy for him. He had so much he had to do to join our team. Coach Marrow was told by Coach LeForce that we were too cocky and he needed to run us hard. Coach Lebo had some running drills that they did at UNC and boy they were tough. We had to run 200 meter dashes and we had a certain amount of time to run them in. We started at 6 and we would work our way all the way up to 16. The first time we did 6, I thought the coaches were crazy, but once we started pacing ourselves it became easier. Well, Loren finally got the okay to join our team and we were on sprint number 10. We liked Loren so we tried to warn him.

I told him, "I know you're excited to be out here, but take my advice, stay with me and we'll help you get through this."

He said "Okay," but when we lined up and that whistle blew, Loren was gone. I thought he was going to set a world record. Major and Alvin looked at me and we started betting which sprint was going to get him. None of the sprints got him. He finished, but afterwards he was lying on the ground and he was seeing stars. When he finally got back to the gym we were already playing and he couldn't believe that. Welcome to ETSU basketball.

The preseason was awesome. Our practices were so intense, it was like a fight could break out at any moment. Coach L. had this drill called "the sissy drill". We always did this drill with Coach Robinson, but with Coach LeForce, we did this drill more. The drill went like this: first, he would roll the ball on the floor and make you dive on it. That made us understand that the wooden floor hurts for a little while but getting the ball makes the pain go away. Second, you had to get up and take a charge from one of our big guys. Then you had to deal with Marty and Calvin holding two blocking pads and you had to score on them. Now their job was to make it tough, but when you're dealing with these two, if you try to be tough, they'll show you that you're not that tough. I became exempt from this drill, so I would sit on the sidelines and stretch while they took and gave a beating to each other. I was called the coach's pet or coach's son, but it didn't bother me. I was used to verbal slander from everyone that doubted me because of my size, and plus the coaches knew I was tough.

One day when we had to do the drill, Rodney decided that if I wasn't doing the drill, he wasn't. Calvin said to Rodney, "They'll send you home. They're not sending Mister home," so Rodney did the drill. One of my funniest memories was when we were doing this rebounding drill, and the coaches told Calvin to run for something he wasn't supposed to. In this rebounding drill, if a person gets an offensive rebound, the person that is boxing him out had to run a full court sprint. Calvin got the rebound over me but the coaches were confused on who was supposed to run. One of the coaches told Calvin he has to run. Well, at first he didn't run and one of the coaches brought it to Coach Leforce's attention. Calvin was heated. He told the coach if he had something to say, say it to him. Of course I had to put my two cents in, telling him to run. I never forgot the chair pulling incident. Before I knew it, we were holding him back from going after one of the coaches. I believe all the coaches were scared. Calvin is a nice guy, super nice guy, but if you get on his bad side, you'd better watch out.

Our senior season was upon us fast. We went from trying to figure college basketball out to being a team that was making noise at the mid major level. Our team chemistry was special. We really wanted to see each other succeed. We got along off the court, and during our practices when things became heated, we never threw punches at each other. That made the respect factor huge for us. Our schedule was the toughest schedule ever played at ETSU. That's just my personal opinion, but a lot of schools didn't want to play us, especially in the dome where we hadn't lost in a year-and-half.

We started our season off with the preseason NIT. This was a great tournament to be in, and if you make it into the Final Four, you get to go to New York City and play at Madison Square Garden where the New York Knicks play professional basketball. I enjoyed playing on television. It gave us a chance to display our skills in front of America. We had our first game against Brigham Young University. They had a freshman that was 7'6", his name was Shawn Bradley. We had Ereck Palmer who was 5'4", so on one court we had the tallest and the shortest players in the nation. Now, BYU was a big strong team that tried to push us around, and I have nothing against Utah, but I was almost sure the only black people that were in the gym played for ETSU. They had a crowd of 10,000 screaming fans and they were ready for the start of the basketball season just like us. That's one thing about this year's team, all the wars we've been through, no one was going to intimidate us. Our practices were so intense. We looked forward to playing in tough places. I actually enjoyed playing on the road as well as at home. BYU was physical. I've never had so many tough screens set on me in a game. With our speed and quickness, we neutralized their power. Calvin and Rodney were dunking, Greg was having issues with the 7'6" Bradley (Greg is 6'11" and still didn't come to his shoulders), but it was a total team effort. I finished with 26 points and 9 assists and we beat them 83-80.

Our next game was in Tucson, where we had to play the Arizona Wildcats, and they always had a good team. We knew if we won this game we would be playing in New York on the big stage. Well, playing on the road was tough for us but we stayed in the game. I got into foul trouble so I had to sit and watch, and what I got to see was my main man, Alvin "Junebug" West, put on a show. He finished with a game high 27 points, and at one point of the game, he scored 15 straight points. I was cheering for him and the rest of the team like crazy. When I did get back into the game, I was hustling to get the basketball, as was one of the players from Arizona. The referee said the ball went out off of me. Not agreeing with the call, I took the gum out of my mouth and threw it on the ground and the ref gave me a technical foul which had me on the bench. Chewing gum made me relax for some reason, and I always chewed gum in high school . When I got to ETSU, Coach Robinson's daughter always made sure that I had some gum before the games. I don't like when refs take control of a game like that, and maybe I should've kept my gum in my mouth, but it was getting stale. The final score was 88-79 Arizona. On top of that, our big guy Greg broke his foot and we would be without him the rest of the year. Talk about a sad day, I was sad for him and for our team because we came in together and we were planning to go out together. When you're a senior you have to take advantage of all opportunities, and Greg was our main offensive scorer. As a player, if one of your horses goes down, somebody or everybody will have to pitch in to make up for that loss. It was great playing with big Greg, but one thing is for sure, the game won't stop and you have to keep pressing forward. Our next game was at home against George Mason University, a team that showed no interest in me at all, so secretively I wanted to really show them what they missed out on. They knew about Greg, so their big guys were thinking they were going to have it easy considering our tallest player was now Darell Jones, and he was 6'8". I learned a long time ago never to underestimate an opponent. They took for granted that we would struggle without Greg. They should've noticed that we had a 16 home game winning streak and our fans were great. I remember at the end of the game I was laughing because George Mason was arguing with each other and they just couldn't believe what was happening. We beat them 105-92.

Next up was Austin Peay. We killed them 103-86, and Eckerd College and Wofford were a no-contest. We just beat them real bad and then we traveled to Virginia to play James Madison. I apologize if I seem a little upset at the schools in Virginia, but they didn't even show a little interest in me. When we played these teams it was personal for me and maybe, just maybe, the next time they have an opportunity to take a 5'7" point guard, they'll remember what I did and give another shorter player a chance. This game was closer. I ended up playing against one of the guys that I played against in high school. My team beat his then and beat them now. The final score was 68-65. I remember during this game, Rodney got a big rebound and instead of passing the ball to me, he did his fancy ball handling and the ball went out of bounds. I told him, "If we lose this game because of that play," and left it at that. The next play, he blocked their shot and got the ball to me. Game over.

We headed up to Cincinnati to play the Bearcats. They had a feisty coach named Bob Huggins and he didn't give us too much respect. Because the pregame speech by Coach LeForce had us ready to play, or at least I thought we were ready, they got off to a fast start jumping out on us 11-0. We knew the game wasn't won in the first half, but coach decided to put Jerry Pelphrey in the game and we went on a 3 point barrage that shocked everyone in the building except us. Cincinnati couldn't recover from it. I almost had a triple double, and for you basketball fans that don't know what that is, it's having double figures in 3 different categories. I had 19 points, 10 assists, and 9 turnovers. The defense they played had me turning the ball over more than I ever did in one game, but we won 90-79. I hate turning the ball over, but when you win, you can deal with it a lot better.

Now the game that we had marked on our schedule ever since Coach Robinson left us to go and coach NC State was upon us. When I tell you, the dome was starting to get packed 2 hours before the game was to start. We had to be ready to play this game. One thing that happened before this game was that we got a break to go home. Coach LeForce told us to do nothing, but when I go home I'm going to play with my boys, and what do I do? I twist my ankle. I call Coach Shulman and tell him and he's like, "Mister, do you know who we're playing in two days?" I said "Of course, I didn't do it on purpose." When I got back, we told Coach LeForce that I did it at practice to stay on his good side, and I saw limited action that game. But it was still a great game. Coach Robinson had a good game plan, to get me into foul trouble and it worked. With me on the bench, once again, Calvin, Alvin, Rodney and Major did their thing. I got back in the game and we won in front of the biggest crowd in ETSU history. The final score was 94-91.

After that win, we had the return match with George Mason. It was always fun for me to play close to home where my family and friends could come and watch me play. George Mason is only 45 minutes from Culpeper, so I knew family and friends would try to make it to this game. We didn't get off to a good start, and we were down 16 at the half. I remember walking back to the our locker room and their big guy B. Tucker asked me,

"Do you think its funny now, Mister? I don't see you laughing now."

I said, "We still have another half to play."

But to answer his question, it's never funny when you're losing at half time and you have a coach that likes to chew you out when the opportunity presents itself. Sure enough, Coach LeForce let us have it, and we came out like gang busters in the second half. My roommate Trazel had a coming out party, so-to-speak. He really stepped it up and this game helped his confidence the rest of the year. He finished with 18 points off the bench and I heated up and finished with 29. My family and friends were happy with the outcome. We got the win and the last laugh. The final score was 96-86 and my mom sent us home with some of her oh so famous fried chicken.

Now we're getting ready for our conference games. We're hot, 9-1 without our big guy and everyone is stepping up. We start the conference games off with ASU. We know they're still not happy with us ending their season, so they're ready, but not ready enough. We beat them 89-70. With Greg not playing, everyone was getting more shots. As an offensive player, anytime you can score more, you're happy with it. For me, I was shooting the ball at a high percentage. When I say 75% from the 3 point line, it's not a typing error. I thank the coaches and Major and Alvin, because staying after our practices and running up and down the court making 3-pointers when you're tired made a difference for me. We beat Liberty pretty well, 86-55. We blew past Furman 95-79. Then we played the Citadel. I remember this game for different reasons. I knew against certain teams the starters weren't going to play to much, so we tried to do what we had to do before the coach took us out of the game. On this night, all the starters were clicking once again. With 12 minutes left in the game, we're up 35 points and Coach LeForce takes us out of the game. Well, the second unit comes in and the next thing we know, the lead starts getting lower and lower. I'm beginning to wonder if the coach is going to put us back in the game but, our guys prevailed and we ended up winning the game 96-76.

So after the game we're in the locker room happy that we had another nice victory. Coach LeForce comes into the locker room and tells us to sit down. Now we're at full attention and the story goes like this, "What's the matter with you guys, you think I'm happy with this type of victory? We should've beaten this team by 40. They were about to give up. They put their scrubs in the game so I put my scrubs in the game…I mean I put the rest of our players in the game and we don't finish the game like we should!" The locker room was so quiet, and when coach walked out of the room, I stood up and pointed at the guys he was talking about and said, "Scrub, scrub, scrub!" and we just started laughing. One of the players was mad and felt like coach shouldn't disrespect them, because they worked hard like us every day. I understood that but it was still funny to me.

I remember so much about that season, we were playing some of our best basketball of the 4 years I'd been there, and Coach Leforce was still not happy. We were 13-1 and getting national attention and he was still on us like it was the preseason. Well the seniors got together and had a meeting with him and asked him to fall back some, which meant take it easy. We told him understood what needed to be done and that we'd been doing it for the last 3 years. He took what we said to heart and eased up.

We played Western Carolina and beat them 93-76. We were hot and rolling, 14-1 and we were finally ranked in the top 20 in America. That was a first for ETSU basketball, and boy that was a great feeling. Sports Illustrated did a nice article on us after the Western Carolina game. This was shaping up to be a dream season, and what better time than our senior year? I remember walking into the supermarket and looking for the issues of Sports Illustrated. For a second I thought we would be on the cover, but we were on the inside, and to see my picture in this issue was nice. We were also on a 13 game winning streak heading to UT-Chattanooga. This was a classic. The game was going back and forth and we had a chance to send the game into overtime, but we missed at the buzzer and they beat us 76-74. Of course Coach LeForce said, "Don't talk to me about being too tough on you guys anymore." I'll get back to that game when they come back to the dome.

The next opponent was VMI and the twins were gone. We crushed them 97-66 at their place, and when we stepped into their arena, those military fans were going crazy. It was borderline hostile, but after the first 10 minutes, they sat back and enjoyed the show. My family came up to this game. That's one thing about my family, when we played close enough for them to see us play, you can best believe that they were there. We were back at home waiting to see what Marshall had this year. One thing was for sure, John Taft was the man. He didn't have enough help though and we beat them 99-88. We stepped out of conference to head to Memphis and play the Memphis Tigers. Now was the time to show people we were the best team in Tennessee, and beating Memphis would solidify it in my eyes. This was a tough game. They had a point guard named Elliot Perry. He was as quick as they come and he was another player that the NBA was talking about. Once again another classic, I remember going out to shoot around before the game. Ereck Palmer was already out there shooting and every time he missed a shot the crowd would get on him. You know how they say all black guys look a like, well they thought he was me and I was laughing. This game was one of the worst officiated games that I've ever played in in my life. When I finally got a chance to watch it on television, even one of the commentators said that on one particular play the referee needed to have his stomach x-rayed to see if he swallowed his whistle. I thought that was funny. We got off to a great start, and once again Calvin was the fire starter. I chipped in, and then Rodney came in. The next thing I know we're up 18, but Memphis, being the fighters that they are, fought back and made the game interesting. Elliot hit a big shot to send the game into overtime. The crowd was really into the game at this point, but we've been battled tested and we know how to win. We finally finished them in overtime with a 105-102 victory. This was my favorite game that I played while at ETSU. I finished with 31 points and 13 assists while Elliot Perry finished with 41. I would like to apologize to Alvin and Major. I know I should've been guarding certain players, but to keep me out of foul trouble they always defended the tough offensive player. Thanks guys.

We headed to ASU to play them the second time and we got rid of them real quick. This game I had a career high of 19 assists to go along with 18 points. The final score was 94-78. After that game we head back home with a 18-2 record and it's time for the rematch against UTC. I was waiting for this game and our fans were too. I went out to shoot around before the game and I noticed a bunch of JC Penney's bags on the seats. I asked one of the fans, "What are the Penney's bags about?" They told me that one of the players for UTC got caught shoplifting. I knew Tyrone just from playing against him. When he came out to shoot, he saw the bags. After we shook hands, I was thinking our fans are wonderful, trying to make light of the situation. I was wondering how Coach LeForce was going to get us ready. Well he was low key considering how bad we wanted some revenge. Well right before he gave his final talk, he had a video that made us so ready to play this game. He didn't have to say anything after we watched it. On the video after they beat us at their place, we walked off the court upset about the loss and Coach Leforce showed us what really happened after we got into the locker room. The cameras kept rolling and we saw how they were dancing like they were at the club or in the Soul Train line. With them celebrating at our expense after the game, it took me back to that old saying about touchdowns, "Act like you've been there before." Well it was our chance to get even, and boy did we take advantage of it. The crowd was pumped, we were pumped, and UTC got stumped, 93-70. I finished with 26 points and 8 assists, and I threw 2 alley-oops to Calvin that made Sports Center highlights.

Belmont was in the wrong place at the wrong time, and I say this because we were playing great, we beat them 110-70, and the Citadel got the same formula. We beat them 101-69. One of the things I remember about this game was that this was Coach LeForce's first time back in this area as a head coach. He had a bunch of family and friends at this game. When the game was over, we were walking off the court and we hear a voice yelling at Coach LeForce trying to get his attention. We look up and it's this big lady.

Coach says, "Yes honey"

And she says "You stink,"

And without thinking Coach says, "And you're fat!"

I never laughed so hard in my life and of course since he knew we heard this, he apologized for his actions.

We were playing well heading into Furman, but their point guard Hal Henderson was tough and lead them to victory. I finished with 31 points, but it wasn't enough and they beat us 104-93. We got back on track against Liberty and made them feel our pain. We beat them 90-49. Our next game was on ESPN and it was at midnight against UNC Charlotte. They were a tough team also, and instead of playing us in the Charlotte Coliseum, they played us at one of their favorite venues, the Mind Shaft. The Mind Shaft was like a high school gym and their all-time record when they play games in this building was 93 wins and only 7 losses. This game being at 12 a.m. was really different from our regular schedule for games. Instead of having curfew at midnight, we had to play basketball at midnight. This wasn't a problem for me because some of the parties that we had in high school turned out to be basketball sessions with car lights on. I always like to go out and shoot before the games because that's how I prepare for games on the road. When I walked in the gym and it was already packed, the crowd started yelling, "Mister Sucks! Mister Sucks!" I was shocked. I was always the fan favorite, so I knew right then that we had to shut them up quick. We were also ranked number 12 in the country, so this made the game more competitive. I remember how hot it was in that small gym and during the second half, I was catching cramps in my calf muscles. During timeouts the trainer was stretching me and making sure I could finish the game. We ended the game with another convincing victory, 96-70. It was nice adding another loss to Mind Shaft.

Our next game was against Western Carolina and we beat them up again 102-78. Now our record is 24-3. Our next game is at Marshall, we've moved up to number 10 in the country and with a win, and some key losses to the teams ahead of us, we might be able to get into the top 10. Well there's nothing wrong with wishful thinking, but they beat us in overtime. It was John Taft's night.

They retired his jersey before the game and since they were on probation, this was their biggest game of the season. John played incredible, pouring in 40 points. I had my career high against them, 37 points and added 9 assists. But I found out, usually when I score a lot of points, we lose, and I don't like losing. The final score was 107-103.

We headed back home for our last regular season game against VMI. The previous 3 years watching the other seniors walk out on the court with their families or whoever they chose to walk out with had me excited when my time came around. I'm so proud of my parents and I couldn't wait to show the dome who my mom and dad were. A lot of emotions happened that night with my parents being there, having the best fans in the world getting to see us play for the last time, knowing that this was it for my class. It was our last home game together and it seemed like it happened so fast. I was last to be called after Major, Alvin, and Mike walked out with their families. After I shake all my teammates' hands, I get to my mom and dad. There's a big bouquet of flowers for mom. My dad is clean. He's always been a sharp dresser and he'll let you know that too. I hug dad and as soon as I get to my mom, she's crying with tears of joy. When my mom cries, it automatically makes me cry, and we're hugging and holding each other and she's telling me how proud of me she is and for me to go out there and let them have it. That's what we did. I didn't miss a single shot that night. I finished with 16 points and 10 assists my last home game. VMI played hard but we beat them 88-76.

That night, Calvin hurt his knee and we didn't know how serious it was at the time. We went through another season of not losing at home and our home winning streak moved up to 31 straight home victories. I told you the fans at the dome were the best. We finished the regular season as champions and we went into the conference tournament with a 25-4 record. Even though we beat some very good teams and had played in the previous two NCAA Tournaments, we still didn't think we would get an automatic bid. In my eyes we had to win the tournament once again. I really didn't want to play in the NIT. I believe we were trend-setters and mid-major conferences started getting more respect. The selection committee started recognizing that our conferences might not have the same television exposure as the big conferences, but we came to play just like they did.

First up in the tournament was the Citadel. Now my mindset as a senior was we have a great record and beat some tough teams. Like the previous 2 years, if we win the tournament we automatically go to the big dance, and if we don't win the tournament we'll play in the Post season NIT, which is like the Junior Varsity tournament for college basketball. I told the guys, "I'm not playing in the NIT, so let's do what we been doing and handle our business." Well that set the tone for this game and we beat the Citadel easily. If you recall, I almost had a triple double against Cincinnati. I had a solid first round game, scoring 21 points, grabbing 10 rebounds, and having 9 assists. That's right basketball fans, the assist leader missed the triple double by one assist, and the thing is, I could've gotten it if my freshman roommate would've passed me the ball. It went like this: when I came out of the game we were winning by 20 points. One of the managers, either Larry Bailey or Franklin Jett, told me I was one assist shy for the triple double. I sometimes felt like they were the coaches. Well I tell coach Shulman and he tells coach LeForce. At first they were like "oh well, we don't need him getting hurt trying to reach individual goals". It wasn't even an individual goal, it was something that I thought would be nice to say I've done, because I never did it in high school. After thinking about it, they put me back in the game. I told the guys, "I need one more assist." So it happens that my roomy Trazel gets a steal and I'm right beside him. We're not even at half court yet, and I'm telling him give it to me, and I'll give it back. But as excited as he was, he kept the ball, dribbled four more times, and did a nice reverse dunk. Since he did all of that, I couldn't even be mad at him and the next dead ball, I was taken out of the game. 'FRESHMEN" The final score was 99-70. Calvin didn't play in this game. We were making sure his knee was going to be okay.

We had to play the waiting game to find out who we would be playing in the semifinals, and the media had grown. Now we are getting to talk to a lot of different people that want to know how we feel about the upcoming game. I told them, "It doesn't take much to get ready at this time of the year." Once we found out we'd be playing UTC, we knew it was going to be a war. I said, "They don't like us and we don't like them and I'm sure this is going to be a good one." We ended up killing UTC. It was a cake walk. This was one of our best performances, everyone played well, and we just blew them out. I was surprised to say the least, but we were playing really good basketball and the end of the season is when you need to be playing your best. The final score was ETSU 104- UTC 71.

We made it back to the finals and once again the media wanted to talk to me and Rodney English. Our finals opponent was ASU, another team that we didn't like and they didn't like us. For some reason though, we got along pretty good with ASU players. Steve Spurlock, Rodney Peele, and Ed Ward were all cool guys. The media asked me what I thought meeting ASU in the finals again, and I told them, "It's always good to get back to the finals, and we look forward to a tough battle with those guys." Then they asked Rodney what he thought and he was very straight forward in his response. He told the media, "If ASU is not ready, we will beat them like we beat our first two opponents." He didn't smile one bit and I'm looking at Rodney like WOW, he's really confident. Then the same reporter asked me,

"What do you think about Rodney's comments?"

I always have my teammates back so I said, "I agree with whatever he said." We walked out of the media room and I told Rodney, "you just gave them bulletin board material and if they weren't ready you can believe that they're ready now ".

He looked at me and said, "They'll need more than bulletin board material." That's one thing I loved about Rodney, he was not going to back down from any challenge.

Lights, camera, action! ESPN is in the building once again and right on press row, I notice some NBA scouts. I figure I'm forever the opportunist, so I put myself on display during shoot around before the game and I start showing them my range. I'm shooting from what would be the NBA 3 point line and it's nothing but net. I wanted to show them that I could shoot far from the basket and still make a high percentage. The thing I was still worried about was my man Calvin's knee. We didn't know if he was going to play. He didn't play the first two games of the tournament but come game time he decided to give it a try. I know he knew how important this game was to us. We were already playing without Greg. But to play with out Calvin, how much can a team take? Once the game started, I got off to a great start, hitting my first four out of five 3-point shots. We never looked back. I remember I was coming down about to shoot another 3 when I saw Calvin running down the right side of the court. I threw it up and he went up and dunked it in. I was thinking he was okay, but the next time down he went up for a rebound, came down wrong, and was taken to the locker room. He didn't play anymore the rest of the season. Once again everyone played hard and played well. Rodney backed up what he said and played terrific. Mike, Alvin, Marty, Trazel, Jerry, Major, Ereck, Darrell and all the other Bucs played and we won our 3rd straight conference tournament 101-82. I finished my last tournament game with 31 points and 13 assists, and got my second tournament MVP trophy.

I never, and I mean never, played the game to get awards, but I knew in the back of mind if I played well, there was some kind of award. Watching Michael Jordan holding trophies and cutting down nets, I wanted to do that. To do it three times in a row with guys that you sweat with, eat with, study with, party with, and win with is one of the best feelings I've ever had as a basketball player.

Now let me ask you this: We steamrolled everyone we played in the tournament this year. We won three games by a combined score of 81 points. To only have Alvin West on the second team All- Tournament team and myself on the first team, tell me how we didn't have at least four more players on the All-Tournament team? It makes you wonder who was on the selection committee. But back to the championship game, this celebration was better than last year's, and it was fun sharing it with all of our family and friends. There was so much blue and gold in the stands that we felt like we now owned Asheville! It was like our second home. My mom and dad always made it up for the tournament.

# Chapter 15:
# The Last Dance

This was the last time I would perform in the NCAA tournament, and it was a dream season for me. As a senior, knowing it would be my last go around, it was truly special. Then we find out for sure that Calvin will not be playing in the NCAA tournament. The dream is now becoming a reality and the NCAA selection committee decided to make us a number 10 seed. They shipped us all the way out to Minnesota where we had to play the University of Iowa. I felt like we were disrespected by the selection committee. I'd like to find out how many top 20 teams got a number 10 seed going into the biggest tournament of the year. Even though we weren't at full strength, we worked hard and deserved better. There, I finally get to vent about that, but what's the sense of crying over spilled milk?

We head out to Minnesota. I'm getting a lot of media time, and I'm enjoying every minute of it. I probably enjoyed it too much. Calvin and Greg still came with us and they still supported us, which is why I love them as teammates. Knowing we would have to go to the biggest war without our main two guns was going to be our toughest task of the season. We were still ready to play. I was playing some of my best basketball. I was averaging 20 points and 9 assists a game, and I was shooting the ball really well. I was shooting 60% from the field, 60% from the 3-point line, and 90% from the free throw line. To top that off, I was leading the nation in assists. We're lining up for the 1st round and the coaches have prepared us for Iowa. I watched them some growing up and I knew they were tough. Sometimes that's all you need for your team to be successful. I picked the wrong time to have an off shooting night, but we were still in it. Rodney stepped up big time. He was the player of the game for us. He finished with 25 points and 12 rebounds. I had 11 points and 13 assists with no turnovers. I made 4 out of 13 shots and it took my shooting percentage down to 59%. I was that close to being the first college player to shoot 60% from the field and from the 3-point line. You always remember your first. I know if I would've shot better, we would've advanced to the next round and then you never know what could've happened. I was feeling bad knowing that I've just played my last college game with the guys that helped me to become a college basketball player. I was sitting in my room and Loren told me we should celebrate a great season and we would be getting another ring. We did and we had a blast in Minnesota.

The awards and accomplishments kept coming after the season. I was player of the year in the Southern Conference and I received the Naismith Award, which goes to the best player in America under 6'0". I also received the Edward Steitz Award, which is given to the best 3-point shooter in America. I received the Bob Waters Award, which is given to the Southern Conference male athlete of the year. I also received All-American honors, 2nd team U.S. basketball writers, NABC 2nd team, Associated Press 3rd team, and Sporting News 3rd team. What a difference 4 years made at ETSU! When I look back on it now, it was the best 4 year period of basketball that I've ever had. To Mike, Alvin, Major, Greg, Marty, Calvin, Mo, Trazel, Ereck, Darrell, Avery, Chad, Rodney Jones, Rodney English, Jerry Pelphrey, James Jacobs and the rest of the Bucs that I didn't name, the coaches, and the super fans of Johnson City: it was a pleasure performing for you guys, and I look forward to the day when I can perform on the sideline as a coach.

# Chapter 16:
# Teammates and Fans

Teammates are like brothers, and I've had the pleasure of playing with some great Teammates. I must say that I didn't like all of my teammates, but as long as you get along on the court, that's what really matters. My high school teammates were great because I grew up with these guys and really got to know them and their families. My teammates in college were great, because as a young man, when you're away from your family and you need someone to be there for you, it's a blessing to be able to trust your teammates with your most intimate secrets. I want to say thank you to my high school teammates: you guys were great, you believed in me before anyone else. My guys Chuck and Earl, you two really helped develop my game as a youngster and for that I'll always be grateful. You know if there's ever anything I can do for you, you can count on me.

I'm going to give you a personal recollection of my college teammates. My senior running mates, I knew that one day our run together would come to an end. I also knew that we would be forever linked because of what we accomplished together. I will always respect you guys, and I really enjoyed getting to know you and your Families. Thank you for helping me in ways that no one else could, unless you were in that locker room, or on that bus, or on that plane, or on that basketball court, or in those dorms or in those clubs, or on that track. I'll take all of those memories with me to the grave. One love to the first Fab 5, until Greg decided he didn't want to finish with us.

Mike Woods was a real team player and was truly under-used in our system. Even good players get caught up in the numbers and that's what happened to Mike. He made me a better player, he loved defending me, and I must say he made things tough for me offensively and defensively. He accepted the challenge every day. Even though I know he didn't like his role and he was going to transfer, I'm glad he stayed. Big ups to you Mike and thank you.

When it comes to big men that can do it all, you don't have to look much further than Greg Dennis. His post-up game was legit, he could shoot the 3 pointer like a guard, he would dunk on you and he probably blocked my shot (help side) more than any other teammate I played with. We knew we could go to him in the crunch and he would deliver. He is still a great friend and I have nothing but love for him.

I knew from the first time I met Major Geer, we were going to be cool friends and even cooler teammates. Major could really shoot the basketball and he didn't shoot it enough. He also helped me stay out of foul trouble by defending the better scoring guard. He defended them very well. We used to go at it during practice. I remember one time he was dribbling the ball and I tried to steal it. Our heads collided and we both had to get stitches, and we were both on the court the next day. Off the court he was one of our barbers and someone I still talk to today. He is underrated when it comes to ETSU basketball.

Alvin West, nicknamed Junebug, and I formed a special bond right from the Beginning. I really enjoyed playing with most of my teammates, but if I had to choose which one I enjoyed playing with the most, I'd have to say it's my man Alvin. He was our loud mouth. He loved talking trash to anyone that would listen. He talked so much trash to me when I arrived that I got used to it and learned from him myself. I remember he hurt his knee and had knee surgery.

When he returned after two weeks, he was back dunking. His mental toughness was second to none. He could shoot too. I remember we were playing Memphis State. As soon as he came into the game he took the first shot that was available and missed. The announcer said Alvin had just missed his 21$^{st}$ straight 3-pointer, but that never bothered him and it never bothered me. I told him to keep shooting and he did. No matter how he was shooting, you can best believe that when the Southern Conference Tournament came around, he would be ready. He always wanted to guard the opposing team's best offensive player. What I liked the most was when we were playing defense, and someone on the other team threw a bad pass, he would steal it and yell out, "Watch your passes!", then take it down the court and finish with a smooth dunk. I love that dude.

I was so glad to come in with a class like ours and accomplish so much in four years. Now that I got my degree, we all graduated. Those guys are special and now I'll talk about the other guys that made a difference in my life also. From what I understand, I wasn't the nicest point guard to play with, and if I said anything crazy to any of my teammates in the heat of the battle, please accept my apologies. Sometimes to get through to guys, you might have to yell and use words you don't normally use.

There's something about big guys and small guys hanging out with each other. I guess it's because we know we need each other. If the big man wants the ball, it's in his best interest to get to know the point guard, and if a point guard wants to get open off the screen and roll, then he needs to get along with his big men. Remember that, point guards. Chad Keller was the coolest white dude I ever played with. He liked rap music and he danced like he was black. He would drive me all the way to Virginia so I could see my family. He also took me to North Carolina to a drag racing competition. You know what kind of atmosphere that was, but we had fun. On the court he was a bruiser. He banged with the best of them and didn't back down from anyone. When he came into the game, I knew it was about to get more physical. He set the best picks, and his mid-range jumper was automatic. It was a pleasure to play with Chad.

Darrell Jones was our finesse big guy that had toughness. I remember when Greg went down, Darrell stepped into the starting lineup and did whatever we asked, for whatever time he played. I remember my senior year in the tournament, he got a steal and went down and dunked on a player from the Citadel and it was nasty. If you read this D, get at me. I'd love to know how you're doing.

Rodney Jones is my big homie. We keep in touch and he's just an all-around great man! He was a two-sport star at ETSU and I made sure I supported him during football season. I know what he did for me my freshman year will never be forgotten. On the court we never got to see how good Avery Marshall could've been because he was injured. If he would've been healthy, I believe he would've helped our program get to the next level. Off the court he was big smooth. I hung out with him because that's where the ladies were. Stay up big homie.

I just smile when I think of Marty Story. We were roommates for 2 years and we had a lot of fun in Davis B127. I don't know why they split us up! Well I have an idea, but I guess I'll keep that between Marty and myself. As a player he was our tough guy. I could see that he got that toughness from his family. I love the Storys, (Marty's family). Marty didn't back down from anyone, considering he was 6'3", 190 pounds and he played the power forward position. I'm sure playing football for the Clemson Tigers made him tough, but I'm glad he decided to come back to ETSU and roll with us. That's my boy for life and I'm sure he knows that. He won 4 rings while at ETSU. There's only two other people I know that have done this and I played with all of them.

I call Trazel Silvers my big little roomie. He was a super teammate, even though I only played with him for one year. He listened, worked hard, and became a big time player by the time he finished his career. I'm sorry he got caught up in some of my drama as a roommate, but I'm sure he learned what not to do. When Coach put him into the game, he produced. I've got nothing but love for Trazel.

I enjoyed Rodney English as a player. He was a competitor and was the best junior college player to ever play ETSU, in my personal opinion. Calvin Talford is simply the best player I played with at ETSU. He did it all but drink alcohol. I remember hanging out with him and he's drinking milk in the club! I never threw an alley-oop pass too high for him. He was super exciting. Other teams thought he was soft. I guess they didn't know he was All-State in football, basketball, baseball and track. He probably could've been a driver on the NASCAR circuit as fast as he drove, and he had a great sense of humor. He won four rings just like Greg and Marty, but the only difference is, he played all four years. They got to sit out a year and still reap the benefits of being a champion. I loved playing with him. He was the best dunker I've ever seen and I knew he was going to bring it every night.

Loren Riddick was the only walk-on I ever played with and he could really shoot. Unfortunately, being behind Major and Alvin, he was in the right place at the wrong time. Off the court he's the friendliest, most outgoing person I ever met. If he could help you, he would, and if you're feeling down, he would lift you up. He's a professional in every aspect. Jerry Pelphrey was a smart ball player and he made the game easy. I enjoyed playing with him and he was probably one of the best shooters I was able to play the pick and pop with. Last but not least, my point guard brothers. I remember the first time Ereck Palmer and I met. He was watching me shoot, and I'm thinking this kid must want an autograph. Then I found out he wanted my position. He was shorter than I was, but he was faster than everyone. He was a patient brother considering he had to wait before he would finally get his chance to play. I know it was tough, but after I graduated he went home with me. He really worked on his game and had a nice senior year. He's my boy, and he helped make me into the player that I've become. Maurice Hayes was really one of my best friends. He made me work on days I didn't want to work. We played a lot of one-on-one. Every time we played, before we started,

He would say, "Today's the day!"

I wasn't paying much attention to him, but one day I finally asked him, "Why are you saying that today's the day?"

He said, "I say today's the day because today's the day I'll beat you one-on-one!"

That day never happened but it made us better, and our friendship is still as strong today as it was 20 years ago.

FANS: All I want to say to the fans of ETSU is THANK YOU, you guys helped us in more ways than you can ever imagine. The Diehls, Saddlers, and Powells were great. I always loved the fact that something I did on the basketball court could make a fan stand up and cheer to their heart's content. It made me so happy! You guys helped us in so many ways. From cheering for us to help us come from behind to win the games, to being so loud that the other team knew they didn't have a chance. You helped by intimidating the referees, because we know how they can be. Last but not least, thank you for giving me the honor to sign thousands upon thousands of autographs. We won 31 straight home games because of you guys, and the next season they added 4 more until the streak came to an end. Always remember, I like winning streaks, not losing streaks.

# Chapter 17:
# The Road to the NBA

The road to the National Basketball Association was a different route for me. Right after we lost to Iowa in the NCAA tournament, I found out that I was invited to the NABC College All Star Game. This game was for college players that weren't still playing in the NCAA tournament. I was one of them. This event took place in Indiana where the Final Four was being played. It was a fun atmosphere. I had people who saw me play during the year and I didn't know who they were, but they were telling me I'd get the MVP of the game. Honestly, in All-Star games, I just wanted to win and score, getting my name in the statistician book. Well, this was the beginning of me finding out what it would take for me to make it to the next level. I didn't play too well in this game. I scored 2 points and they were from the free throw line. I didn't get many opportunities to shoot the ball because these teammates, unlike my ETSU guys, were definitely out for themselves. I would learn from this situation later. The great thing about playing in this tournament was that we got tickets to go to the Final Four. I had always dreamed of playing in the Final Four. To attend one would be fine too, but I saw some guys that wanted to go more than I did, so I looked out for them and they looked out for me. I ended up watching the game in my room with a friend and still enjoyed every minute of it.

The NBA Draft was coming up in 2 months and I felt good about my chances. I was an All-American. I played well against guards that had been drafted or were expected to get drafted, but I still had to go to some other college camps before I would know. I went to the Portsmouth Invitational Tournament in Norfolk, Virginia, and this was a place that I thought I would skip, considering most All-Americans don't have to participate in this tournament. I went and like the All-Star game, once you passed the ball you didn't get it back.

I had agents who wanted to represent me coming to ETSU to talk with me, and I finally signed with Herb Rudoy and Pat Lavine out of Chicago. What made me sign with Herb was that I was at home in the summer and he flew to Virginia to meet my family. It was perfect timing because my mom was making her ever-famous fried chicken. He ate dinner with us and had to hustle back to the airport to go back home. For Herb to meet my family was big for me. I signed and worked with him my whole professional career. Thanks for everything Herb and Pat. I love you guys.

THE DRAFT: I wonder how many All-Americans in the history of the NBA draft didn't get drafted. I know I was one of them, but when you don't play well in the All Star games and you're 5'7", your road will be different. When I didn't get drafted, I got a call from the Indiana Pacers. They wanted me to come and work out for them, and if I played well I would get invited to the Veterans' Camp. I was happy about the opportunity and thought I would do well in Indiana. I remember seeing a player there named Greg Grant. He was a smaller guard like myself and I thought if I ever ran into him I would let him have it. Well, it turns out I would have to eat my words and like it. When I went to Indiana, I didn't prepare myself well and I didn't know what to expect. I let my girlfriend come to the camp with me and I found out that I wouldn't make that mistake again. I found out quickly that what you do in college means nothing at the next level. The first day I played bad, the second day I was catching cramps, and the third day I was called into the president's office and released or cut, which ever sounds better for you. That was the first time that ever happened. I had always made every team I ever tried out for, but they say, there's a first time for everything. I was beginning to realize what type of effort it was going to take if I was to play in the NBA.

The Milwaukee Bucks wanted me to come in and try out with their rookies and free agents, but I decided I wasn't ready for the NBA and wanted to see what the Continental Basketball Association was like. That was the league that developed players to play in the NBA. My agent told me that a team in Australia and a team in Germany wanted me to play for them. It was a guaranteed contract which means I didn't have to try out, I was already on the team. I loved the thought of finally being paid to do what I love. Now it was decision time. Looking at the destinations, I decided to try Germany out. Not only because it was a closer flight, but because my younger brother Kap was in the army stationed in Germany and I felt like we would be close to each other. It turned out that Kap was only 2 hours away from me and driving on the Autobahn where the speed limit is as fast as you want to go, that trip only took 1 hour and half.

# Chapter 18:
# Going Abroad

The team I signed with was called Brandt Hagen, and it was in a small town called Hagen, which is one hour from Frankfurt. Playing basketball in Germany was different. First of all, you have to adjust to the time change, then the language, and then finding your way around a new city. I'm glad my teammates helped me with all of these issues. I quickly adjusted to our coach. He was an American, and some of my teammates had played in the States so their English was pretty good. I was confident in my skills and knew if my new teammates hadn't seen a small point guard do his thing, then they would be in for a pleasant surprise.

I quickly found out that European basketball was different than American basketball. The international rules were different but I would adjust. I remember after our first win, we were celebrating in the locker room. The locker room was small, similar to what the away locker rooms look like when you're the visiting team. One of my teammates sets down a case of Beck's beer in the middle of the floor. This is new to me, and I ask one of my guys,

"Who is the beer for?"

And he said "It's for us."

I was like, "Yeah, right!" and the next thing I know I see another teammate drinking the beer and another teammate in the hallway smoking a cigarette. I knew then, this was professional basketball. I grabbed a beer and it was very tasty. You have to be able to adapt.

Two of my teammates were the big guys and like I said back in college for some reason big guys and point guards get along just fine. I guess since we're not competing for the same position we can tolerate each other. My two big guys were Oliver Herklemann, who played for George Mason University, and Mark Suhr who played for the University of Connecticut. Rimus Kurtinitis was a great shooter from Lithuania and he was the first European to shoot in the NBA 3-point contest. We had many battles after practice. Kirk and his army buddies would come to some of my games whenever he got a chance and I would go and visit him on my off days. I looked forward to doing that as well as playing. I liked my teammates but hanging out with my brother and his boys was more of my style. When they came to our games, they really helped the crowd get going.

We had a pretty good start to the season. Right around Christmas time our team goes to Northern California to play seven college basketball teams. It was at this moment that I said, "If I knew then what I know now, I would've been a totally different basketball player." Coach Kelly had us to set up to play some very good college teams. We played Stanford and they beat us. We played California at Berkley and they beat us. We played University of Nevada Reno and we beat them. That was our only win. Then we played the University of San Francisco. They beat us, but during this game, I didn't know that I would get a second opportunity to play in the NBA. The game against San Fran was our last game before heading back to Germany, so I wanted to play well. I ended up having my best game: 42 points, 14 rebounds, and 8 assists. After the game the Player Personnel Director for the Golden State Warriors came up to me and told me he liked how I played. He wanted to know if I'd be interested in coming back to Oakland to work out with the rookies and free agents. If I did well, I'd play on the summer league team and see what happens. I gave him my agent's number and headed back to Germany knowing that this might be my last chance to get in the NBA. All I prayed for was another opportunity to show what I could do as a basketball player. I was using the German team as a stepping stone to get in the NBA.

I went back working harder than ever, playing with more confidence. I finished the season well. I made the All-Star team and it was nice to have my brother come up and share the experience with me. I was also selected to be in the 3-point contest; this was a big weekend. We just played a game on Thursday and Kap and I celebrated my being in the All-Star game. We had to ride a train the next day to Berlin and I was telling Kap, "I just want to get in the books, so I have to score once." The next thing I know, it's half time. I have 14 points and I'm getting ready for the 3-point competition when the dunk competition is about to go on. Before they allow the pros to do their thing, they bring a mini trampoline and they let anyone from the crowd jump off of this and dunk. Well who do I see in line but Kap, and I'm telling him to be careful and he's saying, "Check me out!" When it's his turn he runs and jumps off the trampoline and misses the dunk, but he hangs on to the rim and lands safely. I remember growing up when he did crazy things, he always landed on his feet. I finished second in the 3-point contest, thanks to my teammate Rimus, but I was voted MVP of the All-Star game and made $3000 extra. We won the game and finished the season making the playoffs. We won our first round game but lost in the second round. The team was wanting me to re-sign with them, but I had bigger fish to fry. We finished the season 23-8. One of my friends told me, "You'll be back." and I said, "NO I WON'T."

# Chapter 19:
# The Association

I'm sitting in the airport and I recognize another guy sitting in the airport. His name is Latrell Spreewell. He was the Warriors number one draft pick that summer and he's getting picked up in a limo. It's nice. I see one of the Warrior representatives and I tell him, "I'm with the Warriors" and he looks at me. They have a nice Honda for me, but it's all good. I'm just waiting for my opportunity. This time around, I told myself, I'm going to be more aggressive, especially on the offensive end. If I don't make it this year, it won't be because I didn't play my best. It will be because the NBA is a high level of basketball and a lot of players who try to make it, don't. I finally get settled in and introduced to some people in the organization. I quickly change clothes and get ready for my first workout. I'm feeling good about myself. I'm in the best shape I've been in. I'm better prepared this time around and I don't have a girlfriend staying with me. You live and you learn. I definitely did. At this point I don't know how everything works, I just continue to thank God for this opportunity.

For the next three days I play with so much confidence and people were starting to take notice. I know my shooting really impressed them. After three days I was told that they wanted me to play on the summer league team. I'm thinking I got cut last year so at least this is something new. I had the feeling I must be getting closer to having my wildest dream come true. I always wanted to play in the NBA. It's the best league to play in, and if you make it, you have to consider yourself one of the best players in the world, if only for one year.

The summer league took place in Utah where the Utah Jazz play. My first summer league game I had 14 points, 8 assists and we won. I was starting to feel more comfortable in my abilities. Three games later, right before the game starts, I see the Warriors head coach Don Nelson sitting in the stands. When I see that, I know I better bring it and I did. After the summer league coach takes me out of the game, I'm sitting down watching and Coach Nelson sits right beside me and gives me a couple of pointers. I'm shocked thinking, "The head coach is talking to me. This must be a good thing, I hope". Right before he goes back into stands he tells me he wants me to come back to Veterans' Camp. I knew what Veterans' Camp was and to be invited back to that, I must be getting closer. No one ever told me what to expect, so I'm learning as I go along.

After the summer league was finished, I got to go back to Virginia and work on my game until it was time to come back to California. When I get back to California, that's when it hits me, this could be it. You either make yourself or you break yourself. I was focused like you wouldn't believe, and we still had a couple of days before everyone was supposed to arrive. Some of the vets arrived early. I remember getting ready to play some pick-up with the guys. I'm tying up my shoes and some dude comes in talking, and I recognize him. This dude is All-Star Tim Hardaway. He's like the best point guard going right now. He also won the Naismith Award his senior year in college, and of course we get matched up right away. Tim's a big time trash-talker. I've always had to deal with trash-talkers. I might even talk a little smack every now and then, but this guy was nonstop. It became comical to me. I know I surprised him our first time playing against each other. I knew this once he figured out I could shoot the ball. You always get a strange look from guys that don't think you can shoot. They let you shoot, and when it keeps going through the nets, it gets their attention. The next day he played me more seriously and he got the better of me that day. When he was leaving he was still talking, saying "This how's it's going to be if you make the team," and I said, "I'll be back." I had to say something.

Finally all the people that have guaranteed contracts start to show up, such as Chris Mullin who played on the dream team, Billy Owens who I played against in college, Chris Gatlin, Vic Alexander, Latrell, and Tim. I would learn quickly that Tim tried to intimidate everyone, and if I allowed him to intimidate me, I wouldn't make the team. As a point guard, which I believe is the toughest position in the game of basketball, game recognizes game. Tim was cocky because he had this one move. It was called the killer cross over. I saw this move up close and personal. It was nasty. He would put the ball between his legs one way and then right when you thought he was going right, he would go left. It was really unstoppable. He was tough, but after seeing I wouldn't back down, he respected me and we became cool the rest of the preseason.

I'm playing pretty good in the preseason games and I'm also understanding that the NBA is big business. We had our own plane, and every seat was like a first-class seat. We stayed in the best hotels and we played in the best arenas. I knew this was something I could get used to. The rookies didn't get rooms by ourselves. We had roommates on the road and my roommate was Kevin Stevenson. He was cool. He was a shooting guard. When we traveled to Minnesota to play the Timberwolves, we both got significant playing time. We lost the game, but what I really remember is sitting in our rooms debating if we should go out or not. We hadn't been out all preseason and we decided to go out. After all, we're grown men. So we're waiting for the elevator to come and it's about 12:30 in the morning. I'm thinking I sure hope none of the coaches will be getting off this elevator and what do you know, the head coach and his two assistants get off the elevator. They look like they've been doing what we're about to do. The first two coaches didn't see us, but the third one did and told the other coaches. Coach Nelson looked as us, and told us, "Don't be out chasing women all night," and headed back to his room.

# Chapter 20:
# The Rookie

When I woke up that morning, I knew some decisions were going to be made. One more preseason game and then I would know what the deal was, but after the game I still didn't know if I made it or not. The next day I'm sitting in the locker room waiting to find out something and in walks Tim. He looks at me and asks me if I made the team. I told him I didn't know yet. He walks over to the phone in the locker room and makes a phone call. The next thing I hear is this, "Hello, this is Tim. Did Keith Jennings make the team?" I'm wondering if this is how I'm going to find out if I made the team or not. He looks at me and gives me the thumbs up, smiling at me. I'm up and running around the locker room. As soon as he gets off the phone, I get on the phone and call my mom and dad and let them know I made it and I'll be sending money home soon. This was the happiest basketball day of my life. I finally made it and I finally stopped hearing that I was too short to make it in basketball.

I only made the minimum my first year but it was more than double the $40,000 I made in Germany. With my first check I found a nice apartment to stay in. I wouldn't learn until Billy Owens came to pick me up in his Mercedes that I was in a bad neighborhood. He told me he wouldn't be coming back to this area. There were good people there, but I did move. I bought a nice Nissan

Pathfinder. As soon as I got it and drove to the airport, I forgot all about it because we were traveling to Utah to play our first game of the season.

We arrive in Utah, and I'm feeling comfortable considering this is where we played our summer league games. I remember running out on the court for lay-up lines and I'm looking all over the arena. It's sold out and that's when it hits me. It's not a dream. I made it! Tears start to form in my eyes I'm so happy! Then I see John Stockton and Karl Malone, two future Hall of Famers and Dream Team players. That snaps me back to reality. Tim is doing his thing against John and I already know that Tim will play a lot if not all the game. I'm wondering if the coach will call my name. Sure enough he calls my name. He yells, "Mister," and I'm like "Oh s^%," ripping my sweat pants and sweatshirt off. I'm sitting at the score table waiting for the next dead ball. I check into the game and get a quick steal for a layup and it's every other time I played. There was nothing on my mind but how can we win, and what can I do to help. We beat Utah on opening night, and that was the first time we beat them at their place in eight years. I finished with 10 points and 6 assists, not bad for an NBA rookie.

We traveled to play the Indiana Pacers. I was looking forward to that game considering they cut me, but it wasn't personal. Then we played a couple of games at home before heading to the east coast to play some of the east coast teams. Our first stop was in Miami, and the first thing I liked was the hotel we were staying at. We had a Jacuzzi in our room and Dan Marino's restaurant was right across the street. I finally get over how nice the rooms are and we head to the arena to get ready for the Miami Heat. I always go out and shoot because this is an NBA experience and I want to take advantage of all the opportunities. Then John Salley is walking towards me. I've been a fan of the NBA when John played with the Pistons and won back-to-back titles. I also liked John when he played for Georgia Tech in college with my boys Mark Price and Bruce Dalrymple. John walks right up to me, gives me a nice handshake, and tells me,

"Welcome to the League." For me that meant a lot. First of all, I didn't think anyone would know me and for him to welcome me into this brotherhood had me smiling all game. It must've done something for my game too, because this game I had my career high 22 points.

I checked into the game, got an open look right away, and nailed it. For me, when the ball goes through the nets and makes a certain sound, I knew I was feeling pretty good. Then I get to the basket and my floater drops over John Salley (Sorry John), and then I know it's about to be a good night if I can stay on the floor. I only missed one shot that game. I was 8 for 9 from the field, I hit four three-pointers, and we beat Miami.

After the game we fly right to Orlando, and get ready for the Magic and this time, I get to play against Shaq Daddy. Before the game, Coach Nelson tells us he'll give $100 to whoever can draw a foul on Shaq. I was trying to tell Shaq before the game I was going to score on him, and he just grabbed my butt so I grabbed his butt. His was way bigger than mine, and we're not funny but this game would end differently for me. I was still playing good minutes. When the coach put me in the game early, I was ready. My buddy Chris Corchiani and I would go at it once again. I was having my way again. I had 14 points and we're in the third quarter. I make a move on Chris and my knee hyper-extends backward. I fall to the ground wondering what has happened. Well two teammates carried me back to the locker room and I missed the rest of the game. After the game when we were on the bus, Coach Nelson asked me how I was feeling. I told him my knee was hurting but I didn't think it was too bad, and he said, "Good, because you're going to start against Charlotte and match up against Mugsy Bogues."

Then I said to him "Coach what about the $100 for the Shaq foul"? I couldn't believe it; he actually reached in his pocket and gave it to me.

We get to Charlotte and my knee wasn't feeling any better, but I had a day to rest and see how it felt on game day. Since Charlotte is not too far from

Johnson City, a lot of friends were coming up to the game. I was excited to see them, but when I went out for shoot around and tried to take my first jump shot, my knee felt bad. I knew I wasn't going to be able to play. I told Coach and he told me that we would evaluate the situation when we got back to California. I was hurt because not only was I going to start my first NBA game, I was getting to play against one of the smallest point guards to play in the NBA. He paved the way for guards like me. Mugsy was very receptive and I appreciated that.

We get back to California and I meet with our doctors. Coach Nelson calls me into his office and I'm sitting down. My knee is starting to feel better and Coach tells me that I've torn my Anterior Cruciate Ligament. I didn't know what that meant so I asked. He said "it's your main knee ligament and you'll miss the rest of the season". I almost fainted. I mean, can you imagine working for something your whole life and then having it stripped from you? I just put my head down so he wouldn't see me crying. He told me that we would try to find the best doctors to do the surgery, I could do my rehab with our strength guy Mark Grabow, and I'll be ready for next year if I'm healthy. Those words made me feel better.

I was beginning to think that this was it for the NBA, but I did what he said. I met with one of the doctors for the Los Angeles Lakers, Dr. Lombardo. He did a great job on my knee. Now I just had to get through the rehabilitation. I was in LA when my brother Kirk was just getting out of the Army. He decided to come and live with me so once again, he's by my side while I'm trying to get my knee to act right. Without Kirk, I wonder if I would've been able to get back. On the days when I thought the pain was too much, Kirk was by my side telling me to stay focused and I did. Thanks Kap.

I finally got past the learning to walk again stage and the bending of the knee stage, and I was able to sit on the bench and learn from some of the best. These 5 players come to mind: #1 Michael Jordan who scorched us for 40 points as the Bulls showed us what team basketball is about. #2 Charles Barkley who was just mean and nasty. He played like no one could stop him and we couldn't. #3 Gary Payton who was the best defensive player I got to watch. He and Tim Hardaway went at it. I thought a fight was going to break out every time between those two. #4 Hakeem the Dream Olajuwon who was so smooth and yet tough at the same time. #5 Reggie Miller who loved taking and making the big shot. He would talk to you and let you know there was nothing you could do about it.

I remember one game at the end of the season. I was just waiting for the game to begin, when our public relations person comes up to me and asked me if I didn't mind speaking to a group of Warrior and 49er fans. I was a little nervous considering I had been sitting out most of the year. Then I asked her who was scheduled to speak,

And she said "Steve Young."

I said, "These people are expecting Steve Young, and you want me to speak to them?"

She looked at me and said, "We were going to give Steve this Warrior jacket, but if you speak you can have it."

Man that jacket was sweet, so I spoke and Steve showed up after I had finished. My dad took good care of that jacket and I still wear it today. We finished that season not making the playoffs, but my rehab was going great. I was back on the court without a brace and was cleared to play in 7 months, just in time to play in the summer league again and see what we could improve on for next year.

# Chapter 21:
# Coming Back From Injury

The summer rolled around fast and being cleared to play again was a great day for me. I headed back to Utah with my teammates that needed the extra work like me. We won the summer league finishing 9-1. During the off season we drafted Chris Webber of the Fab 5 out of the University of Michigan. This guy was a beast. I watched them beat my boys from ETSU in the NCAA tournament after they beat Arizona in the first round. I told Chris he was lucky I wasn't there. I would get to know Chris, and the following that he had by himself alone was impressive. Everywhere we went, I saw more young ladies and women wanting to see and meet C. Webb. Right at that moment I saw what it was like to be around a major star. You know you're big time when you have to have an alias. When people called his room, they must've really known him, because anyone would call and ask the craziest things. I didn't have that problem.

This season was my second time going through a lot of things that rookies had to do. I was a second year player with only eight games of experience. I still worked hard and found out this life was something I could live until the wheels fell off. Our practices were simple, considering we had so many games. It would be nothing to come into practice and Coach N. would say, "If anyone hits a half-court shot, there won't be practice today." As soon as somebody hit that shot we all would run out of the gym before he changed his mind, or they would call us and tell us no practice. I'd go with my brothers and hang out in San Francisco, or go to the dunk courts where the runs were low and we could dunk on them. I really enjoyed those days, but being on the court is what really thrilled me about playing in the NBA.

My second season, I played with confidence. When Coach Nelson put me in the game, he expected me to produce and so did I. I also found out that some of the guys will bet you on the littlest things. For instance, I remember shooting with one of my teammates. He wanted to have a 3-point contest with me. He stopped after I was ahead $275 and then he wanted to write me a check. I told him, "Cash rules, get me that paper!" When we traveled, I felt like I was in Las Vegas. It would be nothing for me to hold the money because I was not going to give away my money when these guys had money to blow. I remember holding $5000 and some of the guys used to walk around with much more. It was funny to me, because you could always tell the sad guy, but they acted like it didn't bother them. Also, this year I was real active in the community. The Warriors paid us to go to schools or Habitat events. I would've done it for free. As a matter of fact, I would play the game for free. Anyone that plays in the NBA and loves the game, I would say they would play for free too.

The team would send a limousine to pick me up, and my brothers would ride with me. I also had another teammate name Chris Gatlin, and the organization liked our chemistry so much, we started our own show called the GAT AND MISTER SHOW. This was a fun time. We went to movies and talked about them. We went to the zoo and talked about it. I remember at the zoo, we were walking around and people were coming up to us telling us we were doing a good job. We would say thanks, and then a bird dropped a little something on Chris's shoulder. I told him it was good luck if a bird shit on you. He didn't think that was too funny.

In the month of February my older brother Man had gotten back into school at Shepherd University. He came to visit us during his spring break. He left West Virginia and it was snowing. When he got to California, the sun was beaming. He told me that when he finished school he would be moving out to California with us, and of course he knew it was all good. I had both of my brothers out there with me and they helped make my life so much easier.

I remember getting the chance to redeem myself. This time when we played the Charlotte Hornets, Coach Nelson gave me the opportunity to start again. I matched up with Mugsy Bogues and we won. I finished with 14 points and 7 assists. Coach Nelson and C. Webb had a verbal disagreement that game. I believe that was the beginning of C. Webb getting traded. After that game, it was great to see some of my friends and family come to support me. One of my best friends, Andrew Kube, ended up coming to this game. We grew up together. He surprised me and I left him some tickets. This was the first time we had seen each other since my boy Greg's bachelor party. Boy, we had fun that night. We quickly caught up at one of Charlotte's finest Gentlemen's Clubs where we saw some of the Hornets. Andrew and I are still best of friends to this day. He doesn't like when I talk trash to him though.

When we played in DC against the Bullets, it was great because I had to come up with 30 tickets for family and friends. I didn't get to play too much that game, but it was nice to see my Virginia family come up and support me. I remember seeing all my boys there. We beat the Bullets too and my mom made some of her famous fried chicken. As soon as I got on the bus, Latrell and C. Webb told me to stop holding out on the chicken. Thanks mom! We won 50 games that year and finished 6th in the Western Conference and made the NBA playoffs.

Our first round opponent was the Phoenix Suns and they had a good team. That year they had Charles Barkley, Kevin Johnson and Dan Majerle. We split with them during the regular season. During one of our wins at home, Nike made a nice commercial for Chris Webber. During that game C. Webb had the ball on the left side of the court and Charles Barkley was running beside him. C. Webb took the ball behind his back and dunked on Sir Charles. The ref called a foul. Since both C. Webb and Spreewell are signed with Nike, they put them in a barber shop and they really clown Charles. Somehow I knew Charles would be ready for this game. I really liked playing in Arizona. I loved their arena, but for some reason I didn't shoot the best there. We lose our first 2 games and we were in both of them. I remember in Game 2 we were down 2 points with under 2 minutes remaining in the game, and I get the rebound. I push the ball up court trying to get a quick basket to tie the game up. I see Tim Hardaway on my left and I know he's going to stop at the 3-point line because he likes taking and making big shots. The Suns are hustling back on defense, and right when I pass the ball to Tim, Dan Marjele sticks his forearm out. The ball hits his forearm and bounces right to one of his teammates. We had to foul and they made their free throws. We lose game 2.

We travel back to Oakland and the crowd is hyped. This is the first home playoff game in 2 years and we believe we can win this one. Well it turns out that this night would be unforgettable for two players. One was C. Webb. He was awarded the Rookie of the Year and he actually dropped his trophy. He was still smiling and I was happy for him. He had the best hands of any big man I ever played with. Two was Charles Barkley. He came out on fire. Everything he shot was going in. He even hit a 3-pointer, that's how much he was feeling it. I'm sure that commercial that Nike was running had him ready. At half time he had 38 points. I was like damn! He was hurting everyone that tried to guard him. I remember late in the 4th quarter when we were making our run at them, we were at the foul line and I was talking to Charles at half court.

He said to me, "You know what little fella, y'all talk a lot of shit, but we're going to sweep y'all tonight."

I said, "It's not happening."

I mean what else could I say to someone that was killing us? Well he was right. They did sweep us and he finished with 56 points. I realized after the loss, this experience was better than anything I could've imagined. The NCAA tournament was great, but there's something about getting paid to do what you love, and we all got a nice bonus check for making the playoffs.

# Chapter 22:
# Last Days as A Warrior

We ended the season on such a positive note that the expectations would be high for the next season. The only problem was that C. Webb was a no show for the training camp. That was tough for us, but the NBA is big business and being on the team and still not knowing what was happening was how it was. I would watch SportsCenter to find out if C. Webb was coming back. In the meantime we're beating good teams, and I'm in the rotation early. We started off 7-1 without our big man in the middle and we're thinking once he does come back it's about to be on. Well he never made it back. He was traded to the Bullets in a 3-player trade. We received Rony Seikaly and he was not the player we needed. He was a good guy though, but no C. Webb. We went from 7-1 to 10-21, plus Tim Hardaway blew his knee out, so he was gone the rest of the season. I did get moved into the starting lineup and took full advantage of the situation, but when you're losing a lot of games, the team gets accustomed to losing. As much as I hate to lose, I was going through the motions. This was the worst team I ever played on, but somehow we still managed to keep it interesting.

Since we weren't winning, I took this opportunity to say hello to some of the stars that you see in movies or televisions shows. My list of favorites goes like this: before playing the LA Lakers, I was out shooting around like I do.

Arsenio Hall came up to me and said hello. He was like, "Mister Jennings is in the house," and I honestly felt like he knew me. I was a fan of his show back in the day. Going into the locker room at halftime, I noticed Denzel Washington sitting at the end of his first row seat. I decided I should at least say hello, so I did and he shook my hand and said,

"What's up Keith?"

I said "YOU" and he laughed.

I was smiling thinking to myself, "I just shook Denzel's hand." Super nice guy! That weekend was great because we had to play the LA Clippers on Sunday, so we stayed in LA during the weekend. One of our teammates, Sean Higgins, knew Wesley Snipes. He got us tickets to Wesley Snipes' premiere party for his movie *Boiling Point*. That's when I realized that LA has some of the sexiest women in the world. I was enjoying myself in the club and it seemed like every woman that walked by was a 10 and I'm not lying. Knowing how Magic ruled that city, I decided not to try and get lucky or I might get lucky the wrong way. I met Woody Harrelson that night too. I also met Bell, Biv, Devoe. They are a singing group formerly known as New Edition. I met Queen Latifah and when I was in New York, I met Spike Lee. He had the nerve to tell me he could post me up. I told Spike, "I'd bust your ass," and he laughed, but he knew it was true. It was fun playing in front of the stars.

Coach Nelson decided he had enough of basketball and called a meeting to tell us that he was stepping down as the coach. He would remain well-off considering he was part owner, so he made away with a good sum of money. Then Bob Lanier, a former NBA great, took over the team. In my personal opinion, he was a better player than coach. There are two things I remember the most about this season. First, my son was born, Keith Jennings Jr. The second was this: one day we had to get ready for practice, and when you're losing, practice is bull shit. Everyone was lazy, and that's how we played in our games, lazy. On this particular day, I was one of the first ones to the gym. I walk into the locker room and who do I see sitting down in one of the lockers? It was Michael Jordan and he's putting on a fresh pair of Air Jordan's. Of course I know Michael but I didn't think he knew me.

I said, "What's up Mike?"

He said, "What's up Keith?"

I asked him, "Are you working out with us today?"

And he said, "Yes, I want to see what I can still do."

He had just retired after winning 3 straight NBA Championships. So even though I didn't get to play against him my rookie year because of my knee issues, I got to practice with the best player ever, in my personal opinion, and it was fun.

I didn't ask for too many autographs throughout my career, but there were 4 I did ask. I never asked for myself. It was for other family and friends. The four autographs I got were: Michael Jordan who signed a hat for my son. My son still has that hat. Charles Barkley signed a poster for my boy Leo, Shaq signed a poster for my nephew Cheese, and Karl Malone signed some shoes for my dad. I think my dad gave them to a kid to wear.

I also remember traveling back to Phoenix to play our last regular season game, and one of my boys named Bugzito went to the game with me. I flew him in and after the game we went out to the club. When we got back to my room, one of my teammates knocks on my door. He says he has a couple of women and needs some help. Before I could say anything, my boy Bugsy is up and gone and comes back one hour later with a great story. Playing in the NBA was the life, even for people who had friends that played in the NBA.

I know that losing 57 games in a season qualifies as a disaster season in my eyes and on top of that, there were two new teams coming into the league, the Toronto Raptors and the Vancouver Grizzlies. What happened was, with the new teams coming, they would have a supplemental draft. Every NBA team got to protect six players that couldn't be drafted. I remember Ed Gregory, the guy that saw me play and gave me the opportunity to try out with the Warriors, called me into his office and told me that I wouldn't be one of the guys protected. He told me not to worry, that I wouldn't get taken in the supplemental draft and I could come back and try out for the team. I was shocked that he felt like that, but the NBA is big business. Then two weeks later, I'm sitting and thinking about how I want to resume my career. I've always been the type of player that wanted to play. I didn't mind sitting on the bench if you were better than me, but if I felt I was better or just as good, being the competitor that I am, it didn't sit well with me.

The NBA had the draft for the expansion teams, and on draft day, I get a call from Isiah Thomas, the president for the Toronto Raptors. He tells me the Raptors are going to draft me with their 4th pick. I was sitting at home with my family and when I got off the phone, I told them, "That was Isiah Thomas and they are going to draft me." We watched the draft on television, and sure enough they took me with their 4th pick. My family was up screaming with joy and so was I! It made me feel so much better considering I didn't get drafted when I came out of college. Take that, Mr. Gregory! I always thought before anyone believes in you, you must believe in yourself.

The NBA went into a lockout, which meant no one could practice, no contracts could be signed, and there were no dealings with any teams until the players and owners reached an agreement. During this time, I had the opportunity to play in Spain and get in shape. Because we didn't expect the lockout to last too long, I went to Madrid, Spain, and played with a team called Estudiantes. Their point guard was hurt so they needed a replacement until he got better. Well I went over there for 2 months and made some good money. That was just as much as I was making with the Warriors in that time period, and it was tax free.

The NBA finished with the lockout and I head back to the States and my agent tells me that things aren't working out with Toronto. That disappointed me but he told me that the Milwaukee Bucks wanted me to come in, so I went there and met with Coach Mike Dunleavy. He told me they would love to have me, but I would be with two other point guards and be a situational player. Of course I didn't like that so I told him I'd think about it. My agent told me that the team in Spain wanted me to come back and finish the year, so I decided since I was playing close to 30 minutes a game that I would go back to Spain. My future wife came over to live with me and we had a ball. I would like to apologize to other people who thought they might've come to Spain but it didn't happen, I'm sorry. I finished the year playing in Spain. The Spanish culture was great. I met some good people there and because they hadn't seen a player like me, I quickly became a crowd favorite. The Spanish people gave me the nickname "CONQUITO," which is a chocolate treat. I took pictures in a matador's outfit, and actually the conquitos were pretty good. They kind of reminded me of M & M's.

The other point guard got healthy and he Spanish. They wanted him to play more so we started splitting time, but when the All-Star game came around, I was voted in for the foreigners and started the game. There were two other players on my team who got invited to the All-Star game. One was an American, Chandler Thompson. He played at Ball State University back in the day and he could really jump, not like Calvin but pretty good. Our Spanish teammate named Alberto Herroros was voted to the Spanish team. We all won awards that evening. I was the 3-point champion, Chandler was the dunk champion, and Alberto was MVP of the All Star game. It was a great weekend. We ended up making the playoffs but we lost in the semi-finals to Barcelona. After being in Spain, I realized the NBA life is better and decided to give it another try.

# Chapter 23:
# The Golden Nugget

I always talked to my dad while I was overseas and he would always ask me if I would ever try out for an NBA team again. At first I didn't know if I would or not, but after playing in Spain, I decided what the heck. I'll give it another try because the perks of being in the NBA were so much better than being overseas. I mean we got our own rooms, we traveled first class, we played in the best arenas, we had great uniforms, shoes, and sweatsuits, and the night life was much better. I missed those things and decided I'd try again. I told my agent and he made a couple of calls. The next thing I know I was in Portland, Oregon working out with the Portland Trailblazers. These guys were young and I had more experience than the point guard they had in at the time. His name was Randolph Childress. He played at Wake Forest and our paths would cross again later. I remember they drafted a young kid out of high school by the name of Jermaine O'Neal. I could see he had talent and thought he would learn a lot playing behind Rasheed Wallace and Gary Trent. We had a nice summer league team and just when I thought I would be coming back to veterans' camp with Portland, my agent calls me and tells me that the Denver Nuggets want me to come to their veterans' camp and the opportunity to make the team would be better.

I leave Portland and go to Denver, Colorado and try out for the Denver Nuggets. This opportunity was good. The returning point guards were Mark Jackson, Jerome Allan and Jeff McGinnis. They also brought in Eric Murdock. We played against each other when he was with the Bucks. I got to know Antonio McDyess, Bryant Stith, and LePhonso Ellis. We worked well together in the practices before we started our preseason games. We had our training camp in San Diego, and I didn't realize how the altitude affected players. I mean, playing in Denver's altitude is one thing, but San Diego hit me like a mack truck. It all started with the conditioning that we did, and I found myself sweating more than usual.

I wasn't going to stop, and then things got competitive, especially with me and Dale Ellis. He was a really good shooter and he had won the NBA 3-point contest. My advantage was, I knew about him, but he didn't know about me and I definitely believe I'm one of the best shooters around! So we're doing this shooting game and he goes first. We're taking 14 shots around the perimeter at the 3-point line. His first round, he hit 10 out of 14 and I hit 12. The second round he hit 12 and I hit 11. When we went around the last time he got cold, he only hit 8, which is still good but I was focused. Because the NBA is a proving ground, I knew I had to prove myself as a shooter at this moment. So I'm going around and I hit my first 6, and I'm holding my follow thru a little longer for personal emphasis. After I hit 4 more, I know I've won but I don't want to miss any more shots and I don't. The guys were like "damn little man can shoot the rock", and my main man Ricky Pierce always told me I was a shooting mf'er.

I finish the drill but noticed on my last 3 shots I was catching a mild cramp in my forearm. Afterwards I tell the coach I need to go to the bathroom and he says "Okay." I'm in the bathroom ready to go #1 and I feel a sneeze coming on. When I sneezed I caught a cramp in my throat and then it went down to my stomach. The next thing I know, I'm lying on the floor in the bathroom. I didn't know what to do. Now the cramps are in my legs and arms, and I thought I was going to pass out, but then the trainer came into the locker room and noticed me. He started putting cold wet paper towels on me and then he got help. They called the ambulance and drove me directly to the hospital where they gave me an IV. I stayed there all night and was released the next day. I've caught cramps before, but none of them scared me like this episode.

We leave from San Diego and head right to Hawaii where we're scheduled to play two games against the LA Lakers, and Shaq is with them now. Kobe is a rookie, but Kobe had a cast on his hand so he didn't play. As soon as Shaq saw me, he came to me and said, "Mister Jennings!" and hugged me. Once again he grabbed my ass so I grabbed his. I don't know why we did this but it was funny. I played solid in the first game, scoring 10 points and having 6 assists against Derek Fisher. The second game, Coach Bickerstaff told me I wasn't going to play but I would start our first home game against Charlotte. So I got to relax, which I didn't mind. I knew a couple of guys from Hawaii, so they took care of me while I was there. One of the things I remember the most was hanging out with one of my teammates. We're sitting in his room, which was a suite, and it was nice. He tells me, he believes he could be a pimp in Hawaii. I was like, "If you say so." The next time I visited his room he had 2 beautiful Hawaiian women in his room and I told him, "You're probably right."

So we head back to the coldness of Denver, but the thin air was so fresh, I enjoyed getting up in the morning to work out. We're getting ready to play Charlotte. I get a chance to talk with Mugsy and then it's tip-off time. We win the tip and I'm running the offense. We get a quick basket from Bryant Stith and then Mugsy has the ball. He's coming at me full speed, so low to the ground and he passes it to one of his teammates. They scored and we inbound the ball to me. I'm racing right back at Mugsy and I make a move to my right. That's when I hear my knee make this popping sound and I knew right then and there, I just tore my left ACL.

I had to sit out the rest of the season, but I knew I had gotten back from my first injury in seven months. I thought it would only take seven months to get through this one. Well I was lazier this time around, and in seven months I wasn't 70%, but I was getting stronger as the days went by. Once the season came to a end, the General Manager called me in for my post-season meeting. The next thing I know my dad is calling me, telling me he's sorry I got released by the Nuggets. I didn't even know. That's how that organization does things. Coach Bickerstaff stepped down during this awful season, and Dick Motta took over the team. He did set a milestone this season. He reached his 1,000[th] career loss, not something I'd like to be known for.

# Chapter 24:
# Parlez Vous Francais?

I was released by the Denver Nuggets and I needed to find employment. I was hoping to get another opportunity with a pro team, but with my knee still not 100%, I wasn't against going back to Europe. I got a call from one of my former teammates, Josh Grant. We played together with the Warriors and he was telling me that he played in France for a team named Le Man. It's also the city where they have the 24 hour races. The coach there wasn't happy with their point guard and asked me if I would be interested in playing with them. I was very interested because I needed a job. This was the first summer that I didn't know where I would be working, and it wouldn't be the last. I talked with the coach. His name was Alain Weise. I didn't know it at the time, but he would become my favorite coach to ever play for.

When I arrived in France we had a friendly scrimmage my first day there. My body was out of whack because of the time difference. At first they told me that I wasn't going to play, but then I find myself dressing out and playing. That was a mistake, because after the game and practice next day, the cramps hit me again. This time I was in a French hospital getting I.V.s in me. The next time we played, I played okay but not great. I did a couple of things that made the coach think I would be fine when I recovered from this injury so he had patience with me. We were only an hour train ride from Paris and I visited there during the weekends when we were off.

We got off to a slow start, or should I say, I got off to a slow start. But each month I was starting to feel a little better. By the end of the year, we were fighting for a playoff spot. We ended up getting the last playoff spot and we had to face Pau Ortez. We beat them once in the regular season, but now it was playoff time. The strange thing about this time for me was, my wife was at home ready to have our first child, and she wanted me home badly. I wanted to be home for it, but it's the playoffs. Our chances of winning were already small, but if I went home, the chances would've been even smaller. I asked the coach though, and he said as soon as the season was over I could leave. Two days before game one happened my sister called me at 3 a.m. When the phone rang I had a feeling what was happening. She told me Rachel went into labor so I called her. She was visiting her family in Pennsylvania and I talked with her while she was going through it. I know it wasn't the same as being there. Trust me, I heard about every birthday, but seeing my baby girl for the first time gave me a source of energy that I didn't know I had. I was also feeling better, so I signed a new contract to play for them the following year, and boy was I ready to tear the league up.

I'm finally back healthy and my body feels great. I remember hearing Michael Jordan say that most basketball players will be playing their best basketball between the ages of 28-30. Well I was 29 and I felt this year was going to be my coming out party in Europe. My boy Josh had left us and got picked up by Pau Ortez, the team that beat us in the playoffs. I knew we would be playing against each other once the season got started, and this year's team was my team. I was better acquainted with the French players. The new American we had was Jason Reese. He was a blue collar worker and he could score. It was fun playing with him and Coach W. didn't change his style of coaching. One of the things I remember about this year was that before every game, the coach would give his pep talk and he would always end it by saying, "Get the ball to Keith."

All my teammates would make fun and say, "When in trouble, get the ball to Keith!"

It didn't bother me though, some perks in life you have to deal with.

We got off to a great start, but I also knew the competition was going to be tougher this year. There were two players that I respected and I knew it was going to be a challenge playing against them. They were Keith Gatlin, who played at the University of Maryland, and Jerome Allen, who played at the University of Pennsylvania. We also got to spend some time together in Denver when I had to sit out. I was looking forward to playing against both of these guys. Jerome was up first. We had to travel to Limoges and play his team on the road. He was ready for that game. I didn't shoot the ball well at all, or it could've been the good defense he was playing. I shot 2-12 and finished with 6 points. Jerome didn't talk trash, but I knew when he came to our place I wouldn't shoot 2-12.

Then we had to play Keith Gatlin's team in Chalon. Keith was a big point guard who was 6'5" and as smooth as could be. Our defensive specialist Makon had to defend him, and Keith went to work dropping 27 points on us. I played better, dropping 23, but his team got the win. When the time came to play these guys again, the MVP race was heating up. All of us were mentioned and the fans in Le Man were incredible. We were beating good teams, and the top teams. When we played Limoges again, I was in a groove. We beat Limoges right before Christmas break. I had 29 points and Jerome fouled out. After the game, we talked. He told me they might not be able to go home for Christmas because of the loss to us. Too bad for them, we were going home. Keith's team came back to town. I fouled out of this one, but we still got the job done. My man Terrence Stansbury did his thing for us, and he didn't even have to do his Statue of Liberty dunk that he made famous in the NBA slam dunk competition in the late 80's.

It was fun being in the running for the MVP award. I never thought about it though. I figured everything would happen regardless of how I was thinking, so I just played. All-Star weekend rolled around right after we played in Paris against Tony Parker. He knows me, and we beat them twice! I was voted in as the starting point guard for the Foreigners. It was a good game. The Frenchies played hard, but we finished them off. The second part of the season was coming. I also was shooting and scoring the basketball at a high level. I found out I'm also in a battle for the scoring title, but I knew once I was healthy, I was going to kill this league.

We're playing our last regular season game at home. I tell Coach W. that I know there's a chance I could win the scoring title, but the team we're playing isn't that tough, so if he felt like I needed some rest, it was all good with me. We had the #6 seed, and that wasn't going to change. Right before our game, I saw where the other player, James Scott, had already played and he finished with 25. I guess the players knew this too, and they were telling me before the game I needed 31 points to win the scoring title. My high scoring game of the season that year was against Asvel and I had 37 in a loss. When I look back on my career, the times I've scored a lot of points, we lost. I didn't want to lose this game, so believe me, it wasn't that important to me. Well, we're up on this team and there's 8 minutes left in the game. Coach calls time out. He's in the huddle and he says, "Keith, you only have 11 points." Do the math. I didn't think it was going to be possible for me to get 31 points so I said, "I'll come out of the game," Coach said, "No, everybody pass the ball to Keith, and Keith, you shoot every time!" I quickly searched the faces of my teammates and they were smiling, looking at me. They were like, "Okay." So I was shooting the ball from everywhere, everytime I touched it. I even shot an airball and that hadn't happened since high school. When it was all said and done, I finished with 31 points and we won the game. My team took me out afterwards and we partied in France that night. I will never forget that moment.

The playoffs were about to begin and we got matched up with our rivals Cholet. We didn't like them and they didn't like us. We had to go to their place for game one, and with their team being the #3 seed, they were pretty confident. So the game is on, as soon as we-win the tip, we score. Then they go on a quick run and the next thing we know, we're down 14-2. We regain our composure but we're still down 10 at the half. We get down again by 14, and then we start to press. We didn't press all year, but for some reason they started turning the ball over, then we would score. The next thing we know we're down 2 with 10 seconds left in the game. Coach W. calls a timeout and he's in the huddle about to draw up a play. I stopped him and told him,

"Coach, let's go for the win."

He looked at me like I was crazy at first and then he said, "Okay, get the ball to Keith and everybody else rebound."

I had a tall player guarding me at the time, but I noticed he was waiting at half court, so I told the in-bounder to roll the ball in slowly so we'd have more time. To my amazement, I didn't have to pick the ball up until I was almost at half court. When I picked it up, my defender must have been thinking a pick-and-roll, so he was looking around while still trying to defend me. I'm thinking, "I'm just inside half court. If I had to shoot it from here, I've made it before but I want to get a little closer so I can still shoot it with confidence." Now the clock is at 5 seconds, and I'm thinking if he backs up one more step, I'm shooting it. I was two steps beyond the NBA 3-point line. He did back up and when he realized I was shooting, he tried to put his hand up, but it was too late.

It was like everything was happening in slow motion. Even the crowd was screaming and yelling until they saw that ball in the air. When it left my hand, it felt good. When the ball swished through the nets, you could've heard a pin drop, but they still had time. They threw the ball in, dribbled up, took one last desperation shot and missed. This was Le Mans' first playoff win in 20 years. Our team ran on the court and they all picked me up, and we were talking shit, especially me. I got caught up in the moment. I was saying, "They didn't think we were ready, they don't know us, they don't know me, I've been through wars," and it was a great feeling. I finished with 24 points that game and we were headed back home for game two.

We get back to our place, and this was the night I found out I was MVP of the League. Every one of our fans had little hand-held fans with a picture of my face on them. You know, the little fans they give you in church when the air conditioner isn't working. It was wild to see so many smiling Mister Jennings faces everywhere. Cholet was hungry. They felt like they were the better team since they were the higher seed. Cameras were flashing while they presented me with the MVP trophy. Of course I shared with my teammates, because without them, I could not do it by myself. It was a nice glass trophy with my picture embossed in it. The players had voted for that award. I received another picture trophy from the coaches that voted me MVP. Game 2 was about to start, and I guess we were too hyped and Cholet snuck into our place and beat us. That would send the series back to their place for game three. The same trash we were talking they were saying now. They said, "We shouldn't be going back to our place." "They messed up." "It's our turn now to close it out." I didn't trip, we beat them once at their place and we could do it again.

We went back to their place and I played one of my best games of the season, finishing with 28 points, 7 rebounds and 7 assists. We won that game and were headed into the second round. The #2 seed Asvel was waiting for us. Asvel had a good team. I had played well against them both times. We beat them at our place and they beat us at their place. We knew this was going to be a tough series. To make a long story short, they beat us in two games. I scored 28 points in game one and 32 in game two. I had the type of season that had other teams in the league wanting me to come play for them and Le Man wanting me to stay. I blame my European agents for this fiasco. I had a certain amount of days to say if I was going to play for another team. That time period ran out. I had agreed to play for Asvel and had signed the contract while I was on a cruise to Bermuda, but it turned out that the contract had messed up in the faxing process. My American agent tells me Real Madrid wants me to come and play for them, and it would've been my best contract ever in Europe. I told him I had already given a verbal agreement to Asvel. He told me not to worry, that I should go to the team that I wanted to go to. I decided to take the money and go to Spain. While this was happening, Le Man told me I was under contract, Asvel told me I was under contract, and I signed a contract with Madrid. So I was supposed to be in three places and play for three teams!

Le Man let me out of the contract. Asvel wanted to ban me from playing in Europe. They said their ticket prices went up once they knew the MVP was going to be playing for them. I knew that was B.S. I went to Madrid and got cut after the fourth game when we were 2-2. That was a whirlwind! I needed to take a breath again just explaining it. So after I was cut, I went home and played with my boys. They always helped me stay focused and keep my game at a high level all the time. I always enjoyed those moments. My boys Frank, Cee, Puff, Matt (just to name a few) helped keep me hungry. Then a team from Turkey named Fenerbache wanted me to come over and finish the rest of the season there. This wasn't a bad deal, considering they paid me in cash. They would bring me my money in a brown paper bag every month. I never got paid that way, but it wasn't a bad deal considering I would only play 6 months with them. Everything was sweet. That team was pretty good, but we weren't in the playoff race at the time. Once we got going, though, we started changing the standings. My first night in Istanbul, we had an earthquake. I slept through it. I didn't know until my man Jerome Robinson is knocking on my door in his underwear. He was talking about, "You didn't get out your apartment!" I was like, "For what?" He said, "We just had an earthquake!" I was like, "Damn, next time knock on your boys door before you roll outside." We laughed.

Turkey was good and bad to me. The things I liked were the money, and the guys from other teams that I got to hang out with. Istanbul had six men's and women's teams with Americans on each team. Jerome Allen, Reggie Freeman, and the other Americans always kicked it on the weekend. We had PlayStation tournaments all the time and I won most of them. I remember our locker rooms were terrible. We didn't have a toilet to sit on. It was in the floor, so you had to balance yourself and it was funny. The team stopped paying us in January. I refused to play until I was paid, so the Americans got paid but the Turkish players didn't. You can imagine how the locker room was, but I didn't have anything to do with that. We ended up making the playoffs. Hedo Turkaglu's team knocked us out of the playoffs. I went home the next day, which I shouldn't have done. They told me they would send me my money but it never arrived. So for all you guys that read this and play overseas or hope to play overseas: Don't leave without all of your money.

# Chapter 25:
# Touring the World

I was waiting for my agent to call me and let me know where I would be playing. This was my life, waiting to see where I would go. For some it's not easy, but for me, I'm such a homebody that being in America and getting to watch the beginning of the college football season was not the worst thing for me. Staying in shape by playing with my boys was what I loved the most. I would rather play basketball with my friends than travel across the country to play basketball, but I'm not dumb; playing overseas is what's paying my bills. I always had to do it by myself. It's tough when you can only depend on you. When it's all said and done, you can only answer for yourself, so you better get ready to do things yourself. My agent in Europe had a team in Russia, and he told me if nothing came across for me, I would play with his team. I've never played in Russia but I knew the basketball wasn't too bad. What made this year really interesting was that we played our games in Russia, but we lived in Italy. This team was bad, not good bad, but bad bad. It was a group of guys that were older and at the end of their careers. Our coach was funny. He didn't speak much English and his knowledge of the game was not good.

I remember living in Italy and everyone would say the pasta is so much better. I didn't think so. We stayed one hour from Milan, so we went there quite a bit. On one occasion, I met Bruce Willis at a club. He was a cool guy and I could tell he was having a great time. I said hello and told him I played basketball. I asked him if he was doing a movie there. He said, "Nope, the paparazzi doesn't bother me over here," and with those lovely fans with him, I didn't bother him any more either. All of our games were like road games. We lived in Italy but we would fly to Russia for our home games. We didn't get to know the crowd and the gym was in a hockey rink, so you know it was cold and we were losing. We got off to a 0-4 start. We played an Italian team that had Manu Ginobli on it. He was nice, but our shooting guard, a guy named Derick Hamilton, gave him the business. We still lost the game and now we're 0-5. Then my agent called and told me a team in France wanted me to come and play for them. The name of that team was Strasbourg. I checked the roster and saw where they had some players on that team that I played against while I was in France the first time. It looked like all they were missing was a point guard. So you know me, I hate losing streaks, and honestly I didn't think it was going to get any better. I decided to head back to France and see how things would be.

We arrived in Strasbourg. This is where the European Parliament meets, so the city turned out to be nice. It was easy meeting my new teammates and they made me feel right at home. Our record was 2-5, and upon my arrival we won 11 straight games. It was fun seeing the looks on their faces. Our next game was back to Asvel where they wanted me banned from playing again in Europe because of the contract drama that we went through. I expected a bunch of boos from the fans, and they didn't disappoint me. When the announcer announced my name, the arena was filled with boos and whistling. When fans in Europe whistle at you or while you're playing, it's not because you're attractive, it's because they don't like what they see. I looked right into the camera and told everyone watching that it wasn't my fault. Unless the French people were lip readers, they might've thought I was telling them off.

The game goes on and we beat Asvel. I finished with 23 points and 8 assists, but one of their players set a hard screen on me and hurt my rotator cuff. This was a different type of pain, but it was on my left shoulder. It didn't affect my shooting too much but it was painful, so painful that our next game I didn't think I could play. The French have a different mentality. The coach told me to at least dress out and maybe the other team would think I was going to play, so they would have to prepare differently. My back-up point guard could play, but there was a big difference in our skill levels. I'm sitting on the bench in my uniform trying to get the guys pumped up, but it's not working. We're down at the half by 12 points. There is nothing wrong with my legs and while watching the game I felt like I could make a difference. I just didn't know how much of a difference.

At halftime I tell the coach to let me play, because I'm the type of player that if I have my uniform on, I'll play.

Coach Vitouex said, "Are you sure?" This is another coach that I didn't really like,

But I said, "Yes I'm sure."

I could already see the energy level pick up. We won this game in overtime and I finished with 10 points and 5 assists. I also got screened on my left side so much. This time the pain was worse, but having a 13-game winning streak was better. The next two days of practice I didn't dress out. Even though we were about to play against my friend Stanley Jackson in Chalon, I decided to sit this one out. I was in a sweatsuit sitting on the bench and I didn't even pack a uniform. The coach knew I wasn't playing in this game and we got smacked by 26. I'm a firm believer that when your body talks, you better listen, even if it means not playing. That's one of the things I learned about myself and it helped my career last a little longer.

We ended the season finishing 4th in the league, and that put us into the playoffs once again. Our first round opponent was a team called Dijon. They had a nice point guard and he was up and coming. When I played against him in the regular season, the thing I remembered the most was that he didn't smell good, but I still had to guard him. Some things you must do, but the playoffs were different. We had the home court advantage and our crowd in Strasbourg was getting better and better with each victory. Any basketball player knows when you win, everyone loves you, but when you lose, you find out who your real fans are. The team offered me a new contract before the playoffs started and I accepted. I was hoping we could keep this team together because we had five Americans on our team and we all got along.

Game 1 I found out that the coaches voted me as MVP of the league. That surprised me, considering I missed our first seven games. That winning streak we went on had to help. I told you from the beginning I like winning streaks, and from the start this was a good one. They came out quick, but I hit a couple of big shots at the end and Brian Howard (who played at N.C. State back in the day when we beat them at their place) played real big and we won. Game 2 was at their place and they got off to a great start. They ended up beating us by 15 points, and I must say their point guard played a better game than I did. The newspapers and reporters were asking if I felt a step slow, and of course I told them no. When you're the top dog, and every night another point guard wants to make his name off of what you accomplished, you get used to them playing at a high level against you. If they don't, they'll catch a beat down. Game 3 was back at our place and as the slogan goes, "Win or go home." The crowd was incredible. We got off to a great start and never looked back. We won game 3 and I finished with 16 points and 7 assists. I told the young point guard to keep working hard, that he could be special.

Round 2, we had to face Asvel again and they had Bill Edwards. He was voted MVP by the players and he was a shooting guard that could flat out shoot. We had to go to their place for game one. They just signed a center that we didn't play against the first time and he made a difference for them. They beat us in game 1, but we liked our chances in game 2. You can imagine my reception going back there was not friendly. Game 2 came down to the final seconds. I put us up 1 late in the game with a 3-pointer. They had the ball with under a minute to go in the game, and their big guy hit a big shot to give them the lead. We never got it back. This was a fun year. Being with all the Americans and winning games excited us all. However, like every organization that wins, instead of giving the guys that help you win the money they deserve, they want to go out and get new players. That doesn't always work.

The next year things had changed. Brian didn't get the contract that he wanted so he left. Paris McGurdy was our defensive stopper. Because of him they called us the "Fight Team." I thought Paris was going to fight someone every game, but it made our defense better. David Robinson was a big guy with a German passport and he also did the dirty work, but they let him go too. We picked up J.R. Reid. He was a former NBA player and he lived in Virginia too. We got along just fine and we picked some new players, but it wasn't the same. This season I started to feel a strange pain in my left hip. I was hurting bad after we practiced and after we played the games. I told our team doctor about it, so we ran tests. They told me I had a vascular necrosis. To put it in nutshell, I wasn't getting enough blood in my hip. They wanted to have the surgery in France, but I felt better having the surgery done in America. That's what I opted to do and that was the end of my season there. They stopped paying my contract, so now I was sitting at home rehabbing my hip, waiting to get healthy so I could play again.

The season was over and Strasbourg was interested in how I was feeling. I knew I wasn't 100%, and if I had to go through two-a-day practices, I knew I wouldn't make it through the season. I told them this, but they didn't want me to do that, so I stayed at home and played the waiting game once again. Another team in France called, named Nancy. In French, Nancy means "grace", and this must've been the team that I needed to play for, because they were struggling and didn't think they would be making the playoffs. They already had two American guards: Adrian Autry who I knew from playing at Syracuse University, and Cory Carr who played at Texas Tech. I knew from being overseas that if they were bringing me in, one of them had to go. Cory was coming back from a knee injury, so they decided to let him go. It was me and Red in the back court. Red was Adrian's nickname and we started playing well together. We had another big fella, his name was Jo Jo Garcia. He played for UTEP in college and he was one of my favorite big men to ever play with. I'm sure our paths will cross again one of these days. Well, Coach Silvan knew my situation and he let me take it easy. I only practiced once a day. I knew I wasn't the same. My hip would still hurt, and at this point I was thinking I might have to retire. I have kids that I want to be able to play with, especially if they want to play basketball, so I was really considering it. We ended up making the playoffs and losing in the first round to my old team Le Man. They had a small point guard and his name was Shawnta Rodgers. He was like a mini tank and he could do it all. We became good friends after that season.

# Chapter 26:
# My Last Days as a Professional Basketball Player

I was wondering how I would feel knowing in my heart that this would be my last year of professional basketball. One thing that's for sure, I knew it was time. It was tough. I've seen a lot of retirements on television and the emotions that go into it seemed overwhelming. I was feeling pretty good about it, and to make things even better, my favorite coach in Europe, Coach Weise, was now the head coach for Strasbourg. He wanted me to play for him. I told him that this would be my last year but he didn't believe me. I told him how I was feeling and he said to do as much as I could in practice, just be ready to play in the games. That was music to my ears. The team was totally different from the team that I played with last time that made the playoffs. We had some veterans, but we also had some young talent that could help us. One of those young guys was Jack Wampler. He was from Cameron, and he told me that when we met the first time I played for Strasbourg and that he worked on everything that I had taught him. He told me that I helped him during that time. He also told me that since he didn't know where I was, that he prayed to God that I would come back to Strasbourg and here I was. God does answer prayers.

So the season is starting and each month I know we're getting closer to finishing the year, and I'm really enjoying myself. We played Asvel and my friend Shawnta changed teams and played for them. My injury was making a difference in how I played, but when you're a veteran like me, you find a way to get through it. I did and we beat Asvel. I had 18 points and 8 assists. After the game Coach W. said, "Are you sure you're going to retire? You can play 2 or 3 more years." I laughed because I really thought I could, but this pain was getting tougher to deal with every time I stepped on the court. I made the All-Star team my last year and it was fun playing with Shawnta in that game. We played together, too, so I'm sure that was the smallest backcourt ever to play in a All-Star game. He's 5'4", I'm 5'7", and our team won.

We ended up getting the 8th seed, which meant when the playoffs started we'd have to play the number one seed. That was Pau Ortez. They had Mikel Peitrus that played with the Golden State Warriors and Boris Diaw that played with the Phoenix Suns, and they were good. The beat us in game one at our place. We had two of our best players hurt, so I really tried to do more, and in doing more, my hip hurt more. They beat us by 11, but after the game, while we were still on the court, the president of our team had a surprise ceremony for me. It was nice. I guess they thought we wouldn't be back to play another game and they wanted to show me how much they appreciated what I'd done. I thought I would be able to hold back the tears, but when you put so much love, so much blood, so much sweat and so many tears in this game and you know it's time to step away from it, you realize how truly blessed you've been to play the game of basketball in front of so many people all over the world. My teammates were picking me up and the arena was chanting my name. I was thinking this is a great send off. I just wish my mom and dad, brothers and sisters and closest friends could've been there to witness this, because when no one believed in me, these people did. The only thing is we had another game to play at their place. The way my hip was feeling, I didn't think I could play on two days' rest. I found a way and we ended up getting beat. It's kind of weird to know that the first time I ever played a playoff game in France I got beat by Pau Ortez, and that's who ended my career. I played okay considering the pain I was in. I finished the night with 14 points and I made my last shot. I don't know why that stuck with me, but being the shooter that I am, anything less than that would be uncivilized. The fans of Pau gave me a standing ovation and this wasn't even my home arena. I guess some fans really appreciate a good basketball player. One of the best compliments Coach W. gave me after I retired was back when I first played for him in Le Man. He said that the season I had when I was the MVP was the best season any American ever had. That was his opinion, and I was happy to hear it.

# Chapter 27:
# Memory Bank

MY TOP 10 BASKETBALL MEMORIES

1.  Making the NBA---a dream come true
2.  Winning the Southern Conference Tournament Championship as a sophomore
3.  Playing in the NBA playoffs
4.  Playing in the NCAA tournament
5.  Cutting down the nets as a sophomore in high school after winning the Battlefield District Tournament
6.  Beating Man in 1-on-1 for the first time as a freshman
7.  4th all-time in assists in NCAA history
8.  My first MVP in France
9.  1st team All-State as a junior
10. Hitting the game-winning shot in Game 1 of the French Playoffs

## MY TOP 5 ARENAS IN AMERICA THAT I PLAYED IN

1. The Mini Dome in Johnson City, Tennessee
2. The Coliseum in Oakland
3. The Delta Center in Salt Lake City, Utah
4. The L.A. Forum
5. Madison Square Garden in New York

## MY TOP 10 PLAYERS I PLAYED WITH IN THE NBA

1. Latrell Spreewell: He was a great teammate. I'd go to war with him anytime.
2. Tim Hardaway: Killer crossover, enough said.
3. Chris Webber: He had the softest hands for a big guy I ever played with.
4. Chris Mullin: He was the best shooter I played with.
5. Billy Owens: He was just smooth.
6. Jeff Grayer: Tough as nails and a great spade partner.
7. Chris Gatlin: He was a great finisher around the basket.
8. Antonio McDyess: He was an incredible leaper in Denver.
9. Mark Jackson: He showed me the art of the setup.
10. Ricky Pierce: He was like a mentor to me.

MY TOP 10 PEOPLE I PLAYED AGAINST IN THE NBA

1. Gary Payton: The Glove

2. Kevin Johnson: Quick point guard for the Suns

3. Charles Barkley: Didn't have to guard and didn't want to

4. Mugsy Bogues: He was so low to the ground and fast.

5. Mark Price: He was just tough.

6. John Stockton: He was just as tough.

7. Scottie Pippen: He controlled everything while Mike was gone.

8. Jason Kidd: I caught him early in Dallas.

9. Rod Strickland: He finished around the basket better than any guard.

10. Terry Dehere: He was a tough post-up guard.

Currently, I'm working for Lees McRae College in Banner Elk NC as an assistant basketball coach for Steve Hardin. He has allowed me to spread my wings as a coach and it's a pleasure to come to work every day working for him and with young super recruiter Daniel Waln. Getting the opportunity to help make a difference with young people is what I'm trying to do. Coach Murray Bartow gave me the opportunity to come back to East Tennessee State to finish my degree. I did and I really appreciated Coach giving me that chance. In the near future I want to be a head basketball coach again. I coached at a private school in Warrenton, Virginia, called Highland School. The kids learned a lot, but I know they really enjoyed learning from a former NBA basketball player.

That's my story, and that's the life I was able to live. I'm sure there are so many more memories, but I just couldn't get to them all. If you ever see me and you want to ask me about this time, feel free to do so. I won't look at you like you're crazy, I just like sharing stories. I would love to thank my family for their undying support. Each one of them has done something to help me accomplish what I did. This will never be forgotten. I'd like to thank Kelly Cole for helping me finish this project and giving me the insight to get it done. I would like to send a personal thank-you to Jim Powell for helping me when the times were tough. Even though I know I could never repay you, you can best believe that I will try.

Peace and Love,
Keith Mister Jennings

This book is dedicated to my Uncle Chuck, thank you for the tough love; I know you're smiling down on me. One love fam.

Made in United States
Orlando, FL
13 June 2022

18760698R00070